CORE BIBLICAL STUDIES

APOCALYPTIC LITERATURE IN THE NEW TESTAMENT

General Editors
Core Biblical Studies
Louis Stulman, *Old Testament*
Warren Carter, *New Testament*

Other Books in the Core Biblical Studies Series
The Apocrypha by David A. deSilva
The Dead Sea Scrolls by Peter Flint

CORE BIBLICAL STUDIES

APOCALYPTIC LITERATURE IN THE NEW TESTAMENT

GREG CAREY

Nashville

APOCALYPTIC LITERATURE IN THE NEW TESTAMENT
Copyright © 2016 by Abingdon Press

All rights reserved.

No part of this work may be reproduced or transmitted in any form or by any means, electronic or mechanical, including photocopying and recording, or by any information storage or retrieval system, except as may be expressly permitted by the 1976 Copyright Act or in writing from the publisher. Requests for permission should be addressed to Permissions, Abingdon Press, 2222 Rosa L. Parks Blvd., PO Box 280988, Nashville, TN 37228-0988, or permissions@umpublishing.org.

This book is printed on acid-free paper.

Library of Congress Cataloging-in-Publication Data

Names: Carey, Greg, 1965- author.
Title: Apocalyptic literature in the New Testament / Greg Carey.
Description: First [edition]. | Nashville, Tennessee : Abingdon Press, 2016.
 | Series: Core biblical studies | Includes index.
Identifiers: LCCN 2016009754 | ISBN 9781426771958 (pbk.)
Subjects: LCSH: Eschatology--Biblical teaching. | Apocalyptic literature. |
 Bible. New Testament--Criticism, interpretation, etc.
Classification: LCC BS2545.E7 C36 2016 | DDC 225/.046--dc23 LC record available at http://lccn.loc.gov/2016009754

Scripture quotations unless noted otherwise are from the Common English Bible. Copyright © 2011 by the Common English Bible. All rights reserved. Used by permission. www.CommonEnglishBible.com.

Scripture quotations marked NRSV are taken from the New Revised Standard Version of the Bible, copyright 1989, Division of Christian Education of the National Council of the Churches of Christ in the United States of America. Used by permission. All rights reserved.

Scripture quotations for the Gospel of Thomas are taken from Bart Ehrman and Zlatko Pleše, *The Other Gospels: Accounts of Jesus from Outside the New Testament* (New York: Oxford University Press, 2014), 161–73.

16 17 18 19 20 21 22 23 24 25—10 9 8 7 6 5 4 3 2 1
MANUFACTURED IN THE UNITED STATES OF AMERICA

for Erin Carey

*They say you can jinx a poem
if you talk about it before it is done.*
    —*Billy Collins, "Madmen"*

Contents

Preface ix

General Preface xiii

Abbreviations xv

Chapter One—A Thought Experiment 1

Chapter Two—Apocalyptic Literature in Context 19

Chapter Three—The Pauline Epistles 43

Chapter Four—The Synoptic Take(s) on Jesus 73

Chapter Five—Beyond the Synoptic Gospels:
   Q, Thomas, John—and Jesus 97

Chapter Six—The Big Show: Revelation 113

Chapter Seven—Epilogue 137

Notes 155

Glossary 159

Subject Index 162

Author Index 165

Index of Ancient Sources 167

Preface

This book aims to introduce readers to New Testament apocalyptic literature, but it has other goals as well. For one thing, I will argue that apocalyptic ideas were fundamental to the emergence of Christianity. One might characterize *all* of the New Testament as apocalyptic literature. Rather than single out the book of Revelation and a few key apocalyptic passages, this book calls attention to the apocalyptic dimension of most New Testament literature.

Second, this book provides guidance and resources for interpreting apocalyptic texts. As you read through this book, you will encounter miniature studies of key texts and themes from various books. The aim is not for readers to absorb my conclusions; instead, I am trying to model how apocalyptic discourse might have been meaningful for ancient audiences and how contemporary readers might find meaning in these texts. One basic theme of this book involves the adaptability of apocalyptic discourse. Early Jews and Christians built all sorts of arguments with apocalyptic logic, and they did so for many different reasons. With these helpful assumptions in mind, contemporary readers can engage these texts in meaningful ways.

A third aim is somewhat indirect: I hope this book enhances readers' openness to and appreciation for the relevance of early Christian apocalyptic literature. Many people routinely dismiss this literature because it uses bizarre imagery (the moon turned to blood—really?), because it seems impossible to decipher, or because it reflects unrealistic fantasy rather than effective engagement with the real world. On the contrary, Jews and Christians turned to apocalyptic discourse precisely to address

Preface

their very this-world problems—and they did so in remarkably creative ways. We will explore apocalyptic literature that fosters political resistance, promotes theological innovation, and addresses community strife, among other functions. We will also introduce frameworks that should prove helpful for appreciating this literature as something other than obscure speculation. If, for example, we think of those bizarre symbols as a kind of poetry, we may then explore how poetry empowers levels of communication inaccessible to ordinary discursive language.

I extend gratitude to Professor Warren Carter of Brite Divinity School at Texas Christian University, who invited me to take on this project and whose wise advice has strengthened it immeasurably. David C. Teel of Abingdon Press has offered collegial encouragement and demonstrated patience above and beyond the call of duty. Abingdon's production editor Katie Johnston has ably guided me through the production process. My graduate instructors at Vanderbilt University have fundamentally shaped this project. My advisor Fernando Segovia challenged me to take account of real, "flesh and blood" readers and to attend to the ethical implications of interpretation. Daniel Patte modeled appreciation for diverse, even conflicting points of view and provided a framework for voicing my own opinion in conversation with others. Mary Tolbert introduced me to resources from the study of literature and rhetoric that shape all of my work; it was she who first suggested I might study apocalyptic literature. And Amy-Jill Levine fostered my study of the primary texts of ancient Judaism and Christianity, especially noncanonical literature, in forming my basic approach to apocalyptic discourse. Countless other colleagues have shaped my basic approach, especially (and in alphabetical order) L. Gregory Bloomquist of Saint Paul University (Ottawa), John J. Collins of Yale Divinity School, David A. deSilva of Ashland Theological Seminary, Lorenzo DiTomasso of Concordia University (Montreal), Lynn R. Huber of Elon University, Carol A. Newsom of Emory University's Candler School of Theology, Stephen D. O'Leary of the University of Southern California, Tina Pippin of Agnes Scott College, Anathea Portier-Young of the Duke University Divinity School, Vernon K. Robbins of Emory University, and David A. Sánchez of Loyola Marymount University. I am grateful to Lancaster Theological Seminary, particularly President Carol Lytch, Dean David Mellott, and the Board of Trustees, who provided a sabbatical leave that made it possible for me to complete this project. Lancaster Seminary students have already tested and improved most of the ideas in this book, and my conversations with colleagues Julia M. O'Brien and Charles F. Melchert continually inform my understanding of this subject matter.

Apocalyptic literature frequently tells the story of justice and peace overcoming chaos and violence, of hope in the midst of conflict. My older daughter, Erin Summers Carey, knows that story better than most and has grown into an adult woman whom I admire. I dedicate this book to her in anticipation of the first birthday of her son, Matthew Bennett Fries-Carey.

General Preface

This book, part of the Core Biblical Studies series, is designed as a starting point for New Testament study.

The volumes that constitute this series function as gateways. They provide entry points into the topics, methods, and contexts that are central to New Testament studies. They open up these areas for inquiry and understanding.

In addition, they are guidebooks for the resulting journey. Each book seeks to introduce its readers to key concepts and information that assist readers in the process of making meaning of New Testament texts. The series takes very seriously the importance of these New Testament texts, recognizing that they have played and continue to play a vital role in the life of faith communities and indeed in the larger society. Accordingly, the series recognizes that important writings need to be understood and wrestled with, and that the task of meaning making is complicated. These volumes seek to be worthy guides for these efforts.

The volumes also map pathways. Previous readers in various contexts and circumstances have created numerous pathways for engaging the New Testament texts. Pathways are methods or sets of questions or perspectives that highlight dimensions of the texts. Some methods focus on the worlds behind the texts, the contexts from which they emerge and especially the circumstances of the faith communities to which they were addressed. Other methods focus on the text itself and the world that the text constructs. And some methods are especially oriented to the locations and interests of readers, the circumstances and commitments that readers bring to the text in interacting with it. The books in this series cannot engage every dimension of the complex mean-making task, but they can lead readers along some of these pathways. And they can point to newer pathways that encourage further explorations relevant to this cultural moment. This difficult and complex task of interpretation is always an unfolding path as readers in different contexts and with diverse concerns and questions interact with the New Testament texts.

A series that can be a gateway, provide a guide, and map pathways provides important resources for readers of the New Testament. This is what these volumes seek to accomplish.

Warren Carter
General Editor

Abbreviations

AYB	Anchor Yale Bible
BETL	Bibliotheca ephemeridum theologicarum lovaniensium
ESEC	Emory Studies in Early Christianity
FAT	Forschungen zum Alten Testament
JSPS	Journal for the Study of the Pseudepigrapha Supplemental Series
NIDB	*New Interpreter's Dictionary of the Bible*
NovTSup	Supplements to *Novum Testamentum*
OTP	*Old Testament Pseudepigrapha*, ed. James H. Charlesworth
SBLSymS	Society of Biblical Literature Symposium Series
StABH	Studies in American Biblical Hermeneutics
WBC	Word Biblical Commentary
WUNT	Wissenschaftliche Untersuchungen zum Neuen Testament

Chapter One
A Thought Experiment

This first chapter introduces several concepts that prepare us to study early Christian apocalyptic literature—terms like *apocalypse* and *apocalypticism*, among others; the emergence of apocalyptic discourse in ancient Judaism, including its presence among the Dead Sea Scrolls; and modern responses to apocalyptic thought among theologians and public thinkers.

But this chapter also aims to persuade you. Many readers assign apocalyptic literature a marginal space within the Bible. Finding apocalyptic ideas to be bizarre, judgmental, or violent, they assume that those ideas stand far removed from Jesus and his ministry. I once had a pastor invite me to lunch to ask, "What's the problem with Revelation?" Revelation surely represents the Bible's most intense expression of apocalyptic discourse; perhaps Revelation is so different from the rest of the New Testament that we should basically ignore it. Alternatively, some might question the relevance of apocalyptic literature: Does its focus on future deliverance encourage devotees to ignore injustice and violence in the present age? The hip-hop group Arrested Development offered this critique of popular religion: "The word 'cope' and the word 'change,' is directly opposite, not the same."[1]

What if apocalyptic discourse stood not at the periphery of early Christianity but near its center? By reflecting on a thought experiment, an imaginary reader who works her way through the entire (Protestant)

Bible from cover to cover, we will argue that apocalyptic topics provided essential resources for early Christian reflection. Moreover, these ideas and literary devices represented fairly new developments within ancient Judaism. They took recognizable shape not in the Jewish Scriptures, or Old Testament, but in the apocalyptic literature some Jews began to produce in the two or three centuries prior to Jesus's birth and career. Finally, these apocalyptic concepts were "fluid": people were still debating their value and meaning throughout the New Testament period—even within the New Testament itself. For that reason, early Christians could adapt apocalyptic discourse in diverse settings, and they could apply it to attain diverse ends.

Just Imagine...

Let's imagine a first-time reader of the Bible. She is an unusual reader: she pays close attention, and she is especially smart. This reader remembers everything she reads, and she understands almost everything. Every once in a while she might perform an internet search or consult a reference dictionary—what's a Philistine, after all?—but let's imagine that she reads through the Bible from Genesis to Revelation, understanding and remembering everything.

For the sake of our thought experiment we'll have to say a little more. She is reading a Protestant Bible. It doesn't matter much which translation she uses. Let's say she's reading the New Revised Standard Version (NRSV), which is the most widely adopted for classroom use. It's far more important that she is using a Protestant Bible. It includes all the books that occur in the Jewish Bible, but in a different order. This Protestant Bible does not include the books we often identify as the Apocrypha: those books appear in Roman Catholic, Greek Orthodox, and Russian Orthodox Bibles. Different Christian communions have different Bibles.

So our reader finishes what we call the Old Testament. The NRSV called it "The Hebrew Scriptures Commonly Called the Old Testament." When she turns from Malachi, the last book of the Protestant Old Testament, she encounters a page, "The New Covenant Commonly Called the

New Testament of Our Lord and Savior Jesus Christ." Then she turns to Matthew.

Now we dwell on that transition to Matthew. Moving from Malachi to Matthew will confront our imaginary reader with several challenges. Matthew begins by introducing Jesus "the Messiah, the son of David, the son of Abraham" (Matt 1:1 NRSV). Our reader recalls David and Abraham as major figures from earlier in the Bible, but what is a messiah?

It's common among some Christians to claim that the Hebrew prophets predicted a messiah, specifically that they predicted Jesus. But our reader finds herself surprised. She looks up "messiah" in a Bible dictionary and finds a fairly lengthy article. According to the article, "messiah" basically means one who is anointed, often kings and sometimes priests or prophets who receive anointing as a sign that one is favored by God for a particular role. She might learn that "*the* Messiah" (with the definite article) occurs in the New Testament but not in the Old Testament. She may also learn that the Greek word we translate "messiah", *christos*, is sometimes translated *messiah* and sometimes *Christ*.

In other words, Matthew calls Jesus "*the* Messiah," a concept that is never fully developed in the Jewish Scriptures. We might offer similar observations regarding other concepts our reader encounters in Matthew. In each case we find that a concept that appears scarcely or not at all in the Old Testament appears with far more definition in the New Testament. And in each case, our best evidence for that process of refinement and definition comes from outside the Bible—in the apocalyptic literature of ancient Judaism. Some of the most basic concepts in early Christian discourse are thoroughly grounded in apocalyptic literature. Messianic speculation emerged from Israel's hopes for a king like David, one who would inaugurate an age of righteousness and peace. Prominent passages include 2 Samuel 7:4-29; 1 Kings 3:6; 8:23-26; Psalms 2; 89; Isaiah 9; 11; 42; and 61.[2] Later authors picked up on the depiction of "one like a Son of Man" in Daniel 7, an apocalypse, and we see the concept developing among some of the Dead Sea Scrolls and in apocalypses like *1 Enoch* (especially chaps. 37–71), *2 Baruch*, and *4 Ezra*.[3]

On several occasions Matthew mentions Jesus's resurrection. But Matthew also includes a debate between Jesus and a group called the Sadducees concerning a general resurrection (Matt 22:23-33; see Mark 12:18-27). The first-century Jewish chronicler Josephus includes rejection of a resurrection and an afterlife among the Sadducees' defining characteristics,[4] as does Acts 23:8. We rarely stop to think about it, but this debate reveals something significant: in Jesus's day the resurrection remained a fairly new and controversial idea.

A modern Bible reader might wonder: How can it be that an authoritative group within first-century Judaism rejected the idea of a resurrection? The answer is fairly simple. The Sadducees revered the Torah, the five books attributed to Moses, but not the other books that came to form the Hebrew Bible. The Torah never mentions resurrection. Nor do any of the other biblical books, at least not explicitly, with the exception of Daniel (though see Isa 26:19). Daniel 12:1-3 discusses a resurrection and a judgment. This is significant for two reasons. First, Daniel 7–12 constitutes one of our earliest literary apocalypses. We encounter the Bible's first clear reference to a resurrection in this classic apocalypse. And second, composed somewhere between 167 and 164 BCE, Daniel likely represents the "latest" book in our Old Testament. Once again we encounter a concept basic to early Christianity that crystalized in the apocalyptic literature of ancient Judaism.

Without belaboring the point, our reader finds two other surprises in Matthew: a personified group of demons headed by "the devil" or "Satan" and belief in a final judgment that separates righteous from unrighteous individuals. The concept of a supernatural "devil" (Greek: *diabolos*) is absent from the Septuagint, the Greek translations of the Old Testament that were popular in the ancient world. There's one exception: at 1 Chronicles 21:1 the Septuagint translates the Hebrew *satan* as "devil" when David is "incited" (CEB) to conduct a census of Israel. This figure, *satan*, shows up two other times in the Jewish Scriptures, obtaining divine permission to torment Job (Job 1–2) and opposing the high priest Joshua in Zechariah 3:1-2. But in Matthew the devil personally tests Jesus (Matt 4:1-11) and heads up a group of demons and wicked angels (Matt 9:34; 25:41). Moreover, while the Hebrew Bible once mentions an "evil spirit" sent by God to torment Saul (1 Sam 16:14), in Matthew demons and "unclean spirits" persecute unfortunate human beings in several cases (e.g., Matt 9:32-34; 10:1; 15:22; 17:14-21). Having read the Old Testament, our reader is scarcely prepared for these menacing characters. However, wicked angels are common characters in the noncanonical apocalyptic literature.

Finally, the Hebrew Bible almost always depicts divine judgment as something that happens within the course of ordinary human events, often to nations and cities as much as to individuals. Again Daniel 12:1-3 provides the one clear exception, and it does not envision a dramatic judgment scene. But in Matthew our reader finds references to "the farthest darkness," a realm where people "will be weeping and grinding their teeth" (Matt 8:12; 22:13; 24:51; 25:30), as well as parables that depict the sorting of the righteous from the unrighteous (13:24-30, 36-43, 47-50; 25:31-46).

We have spent quite some time with our imaginary reader. Having finished the Protestant Old Testament, she encounters several challenging new ideas when she turns to Matthew. These ideas—a single messiah, the resurrection, a devil who leads demons and wicked angels, and a final judgment—prove basic to early Christian literature. But our reader's experience of the Old Testament has scarcely prepared her to understand these concepts. All of them found more definitive expression in the Jewish apocalyptic literature that emerged between the third century BCE and the career of Jesus.

Implications

Our thought experiment suggests several important lessons concerning apocalypticism's presence in the New Testament. First, we meet apocalyptic topics and literary forms all over the New Testament—not just in Revelation, but in the Gospels and epistles as well. When we think of biblical apocalyptic literature, our imaginations immediately conjure the book of Revelation. Indeed, Revelation stands as the Bible's classic expression of apocalyptic thought. This book devotes an entire chapter to Revelation. But apocalyptic discourse is everywhere. It is difficult to imagine early Christianity's formation apart from concepts like a messiah, a resurrection, and a final judgment. Satan and the demons are less prevalent, but they play prominent roles as well. Some early Christian texts are more or less "apocalyptic" than others. As we shall see, the Gospel of Thomas entirely rejects apocalyptic thought. But nearly all the earliest Christian writings reflect heavy apocalyptic influence.

Second, our thought experiment indicates the fluidity of apocalyptic discourse in ancient Judaism and earliest Christianity. By fluidity, we mean that apocalyptic ideas remained fairly new and unsettled in the texts we're considering. They had gained wide acceptance, along with some definition. But things like afterlife hope and a final judgment still required work. For example, what happens to people when they die? We have seen Jesus's debate with the Sadducees concerning the resurrection. Within the New Testament itself we encounter diverse understandings of what lies beyond death. In 1 Corinthians 15 and 1 Thessalonians 4:13-18 Paul expresses the conviction that the dead lie, well, dead until a final resurrection. Paul calls this "sleeping." We see the same idea in Matthew 27:52. But Luke envisions people entering other states immediately after death. For example, Jesus promises his crucified neighbor, "today you will be with me in paradise" (23:43; see 16:22-26).

Finally, we cannot overstate how important apocalyptic ideas were for early Christian reflection regarding Jesus and his significance. Even though the resurrection was a relatively new idea, Jesus's followers rapidly became convinced that God had raised Jesus from the dead. And if God indeed raised Jesus, that conviction empowered reflection concerning Jesus's identity as messiah. We will say more about this in later chapters, but Luke's Gospel may help us imagine how that process would have worked. After the crucifixion the risen Jesus "appears" beside two disciples as they walk—but "they were prevented from recognizing him" (Luke 24:16). They lament the news of Jesus's crucifixion: "we had hoped he was the one who would redeem Israel" (24:21). In other words, they thought Jesus might be the messiah or something similar. Some women who followed Jesus have reported that his tomb is empty and some angels announced his resurrection, but the disciples do not yet believe (24:22-24). As the conversation progresses, Jesus explains how these events relate to his identity:

"Wasn't it necessary for the Christ to suffer these things and then enter into his glory?" (24:26). At this key moment in Luke, the concept of the resurrection reinforces claims concerning Jesus's messianic identity. Apart from apocalyptic discourse, this passage would scarcely make sense.

Concepts and Terminology

Until the 1970s interpreters tossed around the word "apocalyptic" without much attempt at serious definition or analytical precision. "Apocalyptic" referred to the expectation that God would intervene dramatically in history, blessing the righteous and damning the wicked. This model basically took the two biblical apocalypses, Daniel and Revelation, as classic cases. Where other sources resembled Daniel and Revelation, they were considered "apocalyptic." When Jesus discussed the Son of Man's coming or "wars and reports of wars," that counted as apocalyptic. Paul's discourses on the resurrection were apocalyptic.

Throughout the 1970s and 1980s, however, interpreters began working alone and in teams to identify meaningful and consistent understandings of apocalyptic literature. Typically they began with the classic literary apocalypses—not just Daniel and Revelation, but noncanonical apocalypses such as *1 Enoch*, *2* and *3 Baruch*, and *4 Ezra* along with the *Shepherd of Hermas* and the *Apocalypse of Peter*. What concepts and literary devices occurred consistently within this literature? And may we discern patterns within the literature that separate some texts from others? For example, *all* the apocalypses tell a story of a revelatory experience, in which a heavenly guide provides instructions and explanations to the visionary. At the same time, *some* apocalypses focus on the resolution of history, while others emphasize "tours" of heaven and hell and still others combine both features. Familiarity with the literary apocalypses' consistent features prepares us to appreciate the differences among them.

We should avoid making too much of definitions and technical terminology. Nevertheless, the distinctions presented here can prove helpful.

We begin with the term *apocalypse*, which refers to a group of literary works that share many common features. *Apocalypse* derives from the Greek *apokalypsis*, which simply means revelation or unveiling. Here an apocalypse means a narrative that relates a mystical revelation concerning otherworldly affairs. For example, Paul claims to have experienced apocalypses or revelations of his own, but he did not compose a literary apocalypse (2 Cor 12:1-10; Gal 1:12; 2:2). The Protestant canon includes two literary apocalypses, Daniel and Revelation; the name "apocalypse" derives from Revelation's very first word. Catholic and Orthodox Bibles include 2 Esdras; we identify an apocalypse called *4 Ezra*, which constitutes chapters 3–14 of 2 Esdras.

The tradition of great literary apocalypses includes quite a few noncanonical works. Most prominent among these is *1 Enoch*, a composite Jewish apocalypse that contains at least five "books" within the larger work that may have been composed over a period as wide as four centuries. *Enoch* was so influential that it made its way into the Ethiopic Orthodox canon. More copies of *Enoch* appear among the Dead Sea Scrolls than of any other noncanonical work; moreover, the New Testament epistle of Jude quotes *Enoch* as prophecy (14-15), while Enoch influenced Matthew as well (compare *1 Enoch* 98:3 with Matt 13:42, 50; and *1 Enoch* 54:5-6 with Matt 25:41).[5]

> ### Two Jewish Revolts
>
> Apocalyptic literature seems to have made its first big splash during a tumultuous time in Jewish history, the Maccabean Revolt of 167–164 BCE. Jewish sources like the books of the Maccabees portray a regional tyrant, Antiochus IV, who imposed Greek culture upon all the people of his empire. We call this process Hellenization. Some Jews welcomed the innovations, while others rejected them as idolatrous. As tensions escalated, a band of rebels conducted a guerilla war that eventually achieved self-governance for Judea. Daniel and major sections of *1 Enoch* speak directly to this crisis, calling Jews to high levels of faithfulness and promising ultimate deliverance from their oppressors.
>
> The First Jewish Revolt, as it's commonly called, occurred between 66 and 70 CE, and with far different results. (A "second" Jewish revolt occurred from 132 to 135 CE.) Apparent initial success faded as the Romans mustered troops and resources, marched through Galilee and Judea, and eventually besieged and destroyed Jerusalem. A series of Jewish apocalypses, along with the book of Revelation, speaks to this crisis.

A Thought Experiment

The great literary apocalypses required a great deal of time, effort, and textual sophistication. Moreover, two historical crises appear to have inspired waves of apocalyptic writing. Daniel and major sections of *1 Enoch* represent responses to the Antiochene Crisis and Maccabean Revolt of 167–164 BCE, while *4 Ezra*, *2 Baruch*, and *3 Baruch* speak to the trauma caused by Jerusalem's destruction in 70 CE. A wave of Christian apocalypses seems to have emerged in the period from 90 to 150 CE: Revelation, the *Shepherd of Hermas*, the *Apocalypse of Peter*, and the *Ascension of Isaiah*. These early Christian apocalypses all indicate varying degrees of concern with persecution. Two of them, Revelation and *Hermas*, stand as the only literary apocalypses that are not pseudonymous; that is, they do not attribute themselves to a fictitious hero from the past. Other prominent literary works strongly resemble the apocalypses.[6]

Too narrow a focus on the literary apocalypses might prevent us from appreciating the fuller range of *apocalyptic literature* and *apocalyptic discourse*. *Apocalyptic literature* refers to the broad constellation of texts that share a worldview and significant stylistic features with the literary apocalypses. Examples range from works like *Jubilees* that look very much like the literary apocalypses to a letter like 1 Corinthians. Remarkably popular in its day, *Jubilees* retells the biblical story from Genesis 1 to roughly Exodus 24. But *Jubilees* also presents itself as a major revelation, in which God reveals to Moses "what (was) in the beginning and what will occur (in the future), the account of the division of all the days of the Law and the testimony" (1:4, *OTP*). *Jubilees* is very much concerned with issues such as the calendar—essential for observing festivals on the correct dates—and proper celebration of the Sabbath. *Jubilees* also "predicts" Israel's future, including a final judgment and a blessed age to come. *Jubilees* provides a perfect example of apocalyptic literature beyond the boundaries of the literary apocalypses.

But let's consider Paul's first letter to the Corinthians. The letter certainly includes some familiar apocalyptic motifs, the kinds of ideas we find among the apocalypses and other related literature. Paul famously develops a lengthy exposition of the future resurrection (chap. 15), a thoroughly apocalyptic concept. He urges his audience to be aware of the coming judgment that will accompany Jesus's ("the Lord's") arrival (1 Cor 4:5), and he informs them that "God's people will judge the world" just as they will judge angels (6:2-3). Indeed, believers should maintain a cautious humility: "now" their judgment is cloudy, but "then" they will know clearly (1 Cor 13:9-12). Expectations of a future resurrection and a final judgment figure prominently in ancient *apocalyptic discourse*, as did hope for a blessed new age, and Christian apocalyptic discourse featured expectation concerning Jesus's return. In short, 1 Corinthians may not represent an example of "apocalyptic literature," but the concepts that mark "apocalyptic discourse" contribute heavily to Paul's overall argument. While we apply the term apocalyptic literature to literary works that greatly resemble the apocalypses in orientation, apocalyptic discourse points to the more popular use—literary or otherwise—of apocalyptic themes.

To some degree the distinction between apocalyptic literature and apocalyptic discourse creates problems. After all, don't apocalyptic texts include apocalyptic themes or topics? But the distinction helps us remember that some apocalyptic discourse was highly literary, involving intense scribal activity and familiarity with a range of other texts, while apocalyptic discourse also flourished outside of texts and among the vast illiterate majority. If Jesus participated in apocalyptic discourse, as the Gospels suggest he did, he probably did so as a person who could neither read nor write.[7] Likewise, Paul was highly literate, but he drew on apocalyptic ideas while he was discussing other, more mundane issues.

We refer to *apocalypticism* to describe the phenomenon of apocalyptic ideas manifesting themselves in social groups and social contexts. Over the years many apocalyptic groups have attained notoriety, particularly those that expected an imminent climax for history. Students may also encounter closely related terms such as *chiliasm, millennialism,* and *millenarianism*. *Chiliasm* typically refers to the specific belief that at some point in the future Jesus will rule the earth for one thousand years. Rooted in that same belief, the terms *millennialism* and *millenarianism* have grown to include almost any expectation that end-time deliverance will come soon. The overlap and imprecise usage related to these terms can cause confusion for many students.

A Thought Experiment

The typical millenarian pattern portends a period of great suffering, sometimes called a "great tribulation," followed by God's victory over the forces of evil and the inauguration of a blessed new age. The Essenes, who copied and created the Dead Sea Scrolls, seem to have held these expectations. They believed they were enduring a battle between the forces of light and those of darkness, and they created literature that anticipates the crisis attending that battle. The sixteenth-century German Peasants' Revolt carried strong apocalyptic overtones. In the 1840s, upstate New York produced both Joseph Smith, the founder of the Church of Jesus Christ of Latter-day Saints (the Mormons), and William Miller, both of whom promoted distinctive brands of millennialism. The very name Latter-day Saints reflects the millennialist leanings of Joseph Smith, the movement's primary founder. "Visions and revelations guided Smith at every turn," writes Stephen Stein,[8] and Smith reported that an angel revealed to him the location of the *Book of Mormon* and instructed him to translate it. William Miller set out to predict the date of Jesus's return, revising his calculations when they proved inaccurate and eventually landing on a specific date. Thousands of his followers described October 22, 1844, as the "Great Disappointment." More recently Americans have witnessed the tragic outcomes of the Peoples Temple, which led to the deaths of 909 people by cyanide poisoning, and the Branch Davidians, about 80 of whom died in a federal raid of their compound near Waco, Texas.

> **William Miller and the Millerites**
>
> William Miller, an earnest student of the Bible in upstate New York, calculated Jesus's return for the period between March 21, 1843, and March 21, 1844. His teachings gathered followers, the "Millerites."
>
> March 21, 1844, passed, and Miller revised his calculations, settling on October 22, 1844. In anticipation of Jesus's return, some believers left crops in the fields, settled debts, and gave away their property. His followers remembered that day as the "Great Disappointment": "We wept, and wept, until the day dawn," one Millerite recalled.[9]

But apocalypticism need not take such dramatic turns. The Essenes, the apocalyptic sect that left to us the Dead Sea Scrolls, expected apocalyptic deliverance, but they also built their community to last. In a more contemporary context, a visit to pretty much any Christian bookstore will reveal a massive "Bible prophecy" section devoted to end-time speculation. A survey of Christian television or radio is likely to produce similar results. End-time expectation provides one of the most distinctive dimensions of American religiosity. For that matter, end-time speculation marks the canonical Gospels and their presentation of Jesus, along with the letters of Paul the apostle. Most contemporary millenarians are not fomenting revolution.

This book generally avoids relying on technical distinctions among apocalypses, apocalyptic literature and apocalyptic discourse, apocalyptic eschatology, and apocalypticism. However, students will encounter such language in other biblical studies resources—and the distinctions can be helpful. For example, apocalyptic discourse is hardly confined to the apocalypses. It's not even limited to apocalyptic literature; after all, apocalyptic ideas flourished among illiterate people just as they did among the scribes.

Apocalyptic Topics

Apocalyptic texts feature a broad but identifiable range of literary techniques and theological concepts. Drawing from the language of ancient rhetoric, we call these literary devices and religious ideas "topics," or commonplaces. If we recall the distinction between literary apocalypses and other cases of apocalyptic discourse, some—but not necessarily all—of these commonplaces occur in every literary apocalypse. For example, every literary apocalypse describes a visionary experience mediated by a heavenly being. Examples of more popular apocalyptic discourse tend to include more narrow sets of characteristics. Paul's apocalyptic passages do not provide overviews of history, as many literary apocalypses do. However, when we encounter a recognizable cluster of this material, we know we're encountering apocalyptic discourse.

Literary Devices

All of the literary apocalypses concern *visions* in which the visionary receives guidance from a *heavenly intermediary*. The heavenly figures provide both instructions and interpretations of what the visionary has seen. Among other speakers, Daniel encounters the angel Gabriel, who explains his vision: "I am going to tell you what will happen during the time of doom that is coming, because at the appointed time there will be an end" (Dan 8:19). In Revelation John speaks with both Jesus and with angels: the risen Jesus instructs John what to write (Rev 1:11), while on one occasion a heavenly voice commands him to "seal up" what he has heard and "don't write it down" (10:4). Heavenly intermediaries contribute to all the literary apocalypses and to some of the closely related apocalyptic literature. Yet even Paul's enigmatic description of his journey to the third heaven includes a direct word from Jesus (2 Cor 12:9). It remains unclear as to whether that word occurred during his heavenly journey or at another time.

With the exception of two Christian apocalypses, Revelation and the *Shepherd of Hermas*, all of the literary apocalypses employ *pseudonymity*; that is, they all purport to be written by a hero of the distant past rather than by their actual authors. The most glaring examples would be the apocalypses attributed to Enoch, a seventh-generation descendant from Adam! We might be tempted to call them forgeries, for clearly some readers understood these authorship claims literally (see Jude 14). However, I am more inclined to regard these instances of pseudonymity more as useful literary fictions. The apocalypses tend to align themselves with just the right visionary: Enoch has seen the heavenly realms; Ezra is just the right man to dictate books of scripture (and other works); and among the Hebrew prophets Isaiah is the one to have "seen" Jesus.

The classic literary apocalypses employ a device called *ex eventu prophecy*, or prophecy "after the fact." This technique relates closely to pseudonymity. To take one classic example, consider the *Animal Apocalypse* in *1 Enoch* 85–90. Readers who know their biblical history immediately recognize the *Animal Apocalypse* as an allegorical retelling of Israel's story from Abraham through the Maccabean Revolt of 167–164 BCE. As a mythical seventh-generation descendant from Adam, Enoch precedes the vast majority of what he reports; that is, he "predicts" Israel's history. His foretelling includes victory for the Maccabees, opening the way for a final judgment. We encounter a similar case in Daniel 11, which also narrates ancient Near Eastern history through that same historical period; thus, scholars date Daniel to the mid-160s BCE as well. In the Synoptic Gospels Jesus "predicts" wars and rumors of wars (Mark 13:7; Matt 24:6; see Luke 21:9), accompanied by the destruction of Jerusalem's temple. Roman forces destroyed the temple in 70 CE, decades after Jesus's career. By "predicting" past events accurately, *ex eventu prophecy* enhances the authority of its genuine predictions.

Perhaps the best known characteristic of apocalyptic literature involves the presence of striking, often bizarre, *symbols*. Daniel 7 provides a classic example: Daniel watches as a succession of four strange beasts rises from the sea. The first looks like a lion but has eagles' wings; the third resembles a leopard but with four wings and four heads. Revelation's Lamb has seven horns and seven eyes (Rev 5:6), while its Beast has ten horns and seven heads (13:1). Many apocalyptic symbols invite readers to decode their significance—as mentioned already, the part of *1 Enoch* called the *Animal Apocalypse* uses a series of animals to recount Israel's history—while others remain opaque to this day. Certain numbers also figure prominently in the literary apocalypses: within the canon we encounter four beasts in Daniel 7 and four horsemen in Revelation 6, along with Daniel's seven weeks (9:25) and Revelation's seven churches, lampstands, stars, seals, trumpets, bowls, thunders, and so forth.

Theological Concepts

Apocalyptic discourse almost always involves an *alternative reality*, as the "present evil age" (Gal 1:4) gives way to a new age or to an otherworldly reality. We ordinarily associate apocalyptic thought with that first option, the displacement of this era with a new reality in which peace and righteousness prevail. For example, most of Paul's letters begin with a reference to the return of Jesus, the revelation of Jesus, or the day of the Lord (1 Cor 1:7-8; Gal 1:4; Phil 1:6; 1 Thess 1:10). An alternative, or a complement, to this *temporal* dimension of apocalyptic discourse introduces a *spatial* dimension. Several of the apocalypses show no real interest in history but instead explore the realms of heaven and hell. The second-century Christian *Apocalypse of Peter* reports the diverse rewards and punishments of heaven and hell, respectively, with a lot more interest in hell. Others blend temporal and spatial concerns. Revelation, for example, reports both John's ascent into the heavenly throne room and God's ultimate victory over the powers of evil. These factors frequently appear outside the literary apocalypses: Jesus repeatedly speaks about the Son of Man's coming, while Paul describes "visions and revelations [apocalypses]" that include his own journey to the third heaven (2 Cor 12:1-10). In all cases apocalyptic discourse maintains that a future or heavenly reality transcends and defines the troubled times in which mortals live.

Apocalyptic discourse often depicts an end-time scenario in which a *period of crisis and conflict* precedes God's decisive intervention in history. Almost always apocalyptic authors present that period of tribulation as imminent, either emerging or in the immediate future. For example, in Mark and Matthew, but not Luke, Jesus sets forth a period of crisis, or "suffering" (Mark 13:19, 24; see Matt 24:21, 29), warning that "this generation won't pass away until all these things happen" (Mark 13:30; see Matt 24:34). This crisis pattern reflects a critical dimension of apocalyptic and millennial movements: they tend to interpret their present moment as the decisive moment in history. The crisis of the present age, whatever concerns prompt apocalyptic authors and speakers to communicate, takes on an ultimate value.

In comparison with other biblical literature, apocalyptic discourse is marked by a combination of *individualism, dualism,* and *determinism.* The concept of divine judgment runs throughout the Bible. In the prophetic tradition it typically (but not always) treats peoples as collectives. That is, God judges cities and nations just as much as God judges individuals. The righteous and the wicked suffer together. Apocalyptic literature, however, distinguishes between righteous and wicked individuals. Moreover, apocalyptic literature tends to make a rigid distinction between righteous and unrighteous persons, as well as righteous and unrighteous supernatural beings, and even between the present wicked age and the blessed age to come. We call this distinction dualism, and it relates to the concept of determinism. Apocalyptic literature typically portrays the fate of mortals and angels as predetermined, as is the course of history. We find a classic example of individualism, dualism, and determinism in Daniel 12. At the end "many" who sleep in the earth will awake, some to life and some to shame (Dan 12:2). In this division the wicked continue to act wickedly because they do not understand. Only the wise understand (Dan 12:10).

Finally, the concepts of *resurrection*, *judgment*, and an *afterlife* also hold prominent places in apocalyptic literature. We have already observed how these concepts remained both new and controversial even during Jesus's career. *First Enoch*'s beginning section, the *Book of the Watchers* (chaps. 1–36), explores the places of punishment designated for those wicked angels ("watchers") who impregnated mortal women, leading to a race of giants and to widespread violence and injustice. (See the story in Gen 6:1-4.) The same section of *1 Enoch* provides a tour of the underworld (chaps. 21–22), where the dead await their final judgment. Even in this intermediate state the righteous have access to fresh water while the wicked endure pain. Ancient Jewish and Christian literature includes a wide range of beliefs concerning such matters. Does death immediately usher people to their ultimate fates, or does an intermediate state await them? In the afterlife do the dead inhabit bodies of any kind? Do the wicked receive eternal punishment or simple destruction? Despite this diversity the question of what lies beyond death inhabits many apocalyptic texts.[10]

What to Expect

This introductory chapter has set out to do two things. First, our thought experiment demonstrates the essential contribution of apocalyptic discourse to the emergence of early Christianity and to its literature. Some may find apocalyptic discourse to be bizarre, boring, objectionable, or irrelevant, yet it is all but impossible to imagine the ministry of Jesus, the composition of the Gospels, the work of Paul, or other dimensions of the New Testament without the emergence of those ideas.

Second, we provided some key terms and categories that will assist us in exploring the New Testament's apocalyptic dimensions. This book generally refrains from technical terminology, but readers who read beyond this volume will encounter these concepts frequently. For example, the New Testament includes only one literary *apocalypse*, but *apocalyptic discourse* occurs throughout the New Testament gospels and epistles. Early Christians who may never have encountered an apocalypse still experienced the influence of that literary movement.

Remarkable creativity and diversity marked early Christian apocalyptic discourse. The rest of this book will return to this concept over and over again. Early Christians turned to the resources of apocalyptic discourse when they faced emerging questions and challenges, often improvising new and important responses to diverse situations. Many readers will assume that apocalyptic discourse simply served to encourage and to threaten audiences—and it often did. On the one hand, hope for Jesus's imminent return could inspire believers to persevere through hard times; on the other hand, the judgment that would accompany Jesus's return might motivate people toward higher levels of faithfulness. But early Christians were far more creative than such a narrow understanding might assume, using apocalyptic ideas to address vexing theological questions, justify social innovation, offer political resistance, and more. Throughout this book we will consider *why* and *how* early Christian authors drew upon apocalyptic discourse. As we move ahead we will encounter the diversity that also characterizes the New Testament. Matthew and Luke use apocalyptic concepts in very different ways. As his ministry progressed Paul seems to have evolved in his understanding of key ideas. Revelation turns apocalyptic discourse to promote ideas that Paul explicitly rejects. This combination of creativity and diversity will guide us throughout this study.

For Further Reading

Bauckham, Richard. *The Fate of the Dead: Studies on the Jewish and Christian Apocalypses.* NovTSup 93. Leiden: Brill, 1998.

Bauckham, Richard, and Trevor Hart. *Hope Against Hope: Christian Eschatology at the Turn of the Millennium.* Grand Rapids: Eerdmans, 1999.

Carey, Greg. *Ultimate Things: An Introduction to Jewish and Christian Apocalyptic Literature.* St. Louis: Chalice Press, 2005.

Clark-Soles, Jaime. *Death and the Afterlife in the New Testament.* New York: T and T Clark, 2006.

Collins, Adela Yarbro, and John J. Collins. *King and Messiah as Son of God: Divine, Human, and Angelic Messianic Figures in Biblical and Related Literature.* Grand Rapids: Eerdmans, 2008.

Collins, John J. *The Apocalyptic Imagination: An Introduction to Jewish Apocalyptic Literature.* 2nd ed. Grand Rapids: Eerdmans, 1998.

———, ed. *The Oxford Handbook of Apocalyptic Literature.* New York: Oxford University Press, 2014.

Hill, Craig C. *In God's Time: The Bible and the Future.* Grand Rapids: Eerdmans, 2002.

Himmelfarb, Martha. *The Apocalypse: A Brief History.* Chichester, England: Wiley-Blackwell, 2010.

Horsley, Richard A. *Scribes, Visionaries, and the Politics of Second Temple Judea.* Louisville: Westminster John Knox Press, 2007.

O'Leary, Stephen D. *Arguing the Apocalypse: A Theory of Millennial Rhetoric.* New York: Oxford University Press, 1994.

Richter, Amy E. *Enoch and the Gospel of Matthew.* Princeton Theological Monographs. Eugene, OR: Wipf & Stock, 2012.

Portier-Young, Anathea E. *Apocalypse Against Empire: Theologies of Resistance in Early Judaism.* Grand Rapids: Eerdmans, 2011.

Segal, Alan F. *Life after Death: A History of the Afterlife in Western Religion.* New York: Doubleday, 2004.

Stein, Stephen J. "Apocalypticism Outside the Mainstream in the United States." Pages 108–39 in *The Encyclopedia of Apocalypticism, Volume 3: Apocalypticism in the Modern Period and the Contemporary Age.* Edited by Stephen J. Stein. New York: Continuum, 2000.

Wright, N. T. *The New Testament and the People of God.* Minneapolis: Fortress Press, 1992.

Chapter Two

Apocalyptic Literature in Context

The primary literary context for interpreting early Christian apocalyptic literature lies in the Jewish literature produced in the second and first centuries BCE and the first century CE. That literature indicates a general stream from which the distinctive concerns and literary techniques of early Christian authors (and speakers) bubbled forth. This chapter sketches some of the antecedents for Jewish apocalyptic literature in earlier periods, often called "proto-apocalyptic" literature, then surveys a sample of the Jewish literature that proves most important for understanding New Testament apocalyptic literature.[1]

Where Did It Come From?

Judaism emerged from a confluence of great and diverse cultures: Egyptian, Phoenician, Ugaritic, Assyrian, Babylonian, Median, Persian, Greek, and Roman, to name the most prominent examples. Naturally, historians have mounted many attempts to explain the origins of apocalyptic literature in terms of cross-cultural influence. For example, some of the literary apocalypses provide overviews of Israel's history in terms of a series of distinct periods, a literary pattern familiar from ancient Persian religion. Persian influence is likely, but other ancient cultures also developed periodic schemes for interpreting history.[2] The apocalypses' interest in otherworldly spaces, particularly the dwelling places of the dead, has parallels from Rome to Greece to Ugarit to Egypt. Countless college students have encountered the visit to the dead in the *Epic of Gilgamesh*, and the heavenly tour in *1 Enoch* 17–19, for example, reflects influence from Homer's *Iliad*.[3]

To put a fine point on things, apocalyptic literature cannot be traced directly to a single ancient culture. We might track the influence of a single text or motif from one source to another, but cultural influence typically works in complicated ways. Rarely does a phenomenon as rich and diverse as apocalyptic literature derive from a single cultural source. Great rivers result from the convergence of many tributaries.

We might say something similar regarding attempts to track apocalyptic literature's Jewish pedigree. Apocalyptic discourse holds a great deal in common with biblical prophecy, particularly the delivery of divine messages through specially appointed mortals. Indeed, we often talk about "proto-apocalyptic" literature. Sections of prophetic books like Isaiah, Ezekiel, Joel, and Zechariah, among others, include concepts and literary devices that later mark the classic Jewish apocalypses. Isaiah includes visions of the divine throne room (Isa 6:1-13) and of cosmic catastrophe (24:17-23). The vision of the dry bones in Ezekiel 37 leads us to wonder whether a belief in resurrection lies in play, while Ezekiel devotes a very long section (chaps. 40–48) to a description of the heavenly temple. Joel characterizes a locust plague in terms of "the day of the LORD" (Joel 2:1-2). Meanwhile, some sections of Zechariah feature visions interpreted by an angel (Zech 1:7–6:8), while other parts envision a violent end-time crisis (chaps. 12–14). At the other end of the historical continuum, Revelation explicitly describes itself as a prophecy (Rev 1:3; 22:7, 10, 18-19).

The ties between apocalyptic and prophetic literature are both obvious and profound, with Hebrew prophetic literature providing an essential resource for the apocalyptic writers. Daniel 9:24 features the remarkable phrase "both vision and prophet" (NRSV), vaguely linking prophecy and vision.[4] As just noted, the author of Revelation repeatedly refers to his work as a prophecy, but otherwise New Testament authors do not label apocalyptic topics in terms of prophecy. John draws heavily upon the prophets for its language and imagery, especially Isaiah and Ezekiel. (Revelation also draws heavily upon Daniel, but in the Jewish canon Daniel is not considered a prophetic book.) We do encounter one remarkable case outside the canon: *The Ascension of Isaiah*, an early Christian apocalypse from the second century BCE, places its apocalyptic revelations in the mouth of one of Israel's greatest prophets. The great Jewish apocalypse *4 Ezra* (found as chaps. 3–14 of 2 Esdras in the Apocrypha) links its revelation to prophecy (*4 Ezra* 7:130) and identifies its protagonist as a prophet (*4 Ezra* 12:42). The link between biblical prophecy and apocalyptic literature goes much deeper than such simple labeling. It lies in the ways in which apocalyptic literature draws from the literary devices and theological outlooks of the biblical prophetic traditions. We see these tendencies most clearly in sections of Isaiah, Ezekiel, Joel, and Zechariah.

Earlier generations of scholars tended to emphasize sharp distinctions between prophetic and apocalyptic literature. They acknowledged that apocalyptic discourse had prophetic roots; however, they believed that the emergence of proto-apocalyptic texts reflected a radical shift in orientation. Where the biblical prophets expressed hope and judgment related to very this-worldly situations, according to this model the proto-apocalyptic texts abandoned hope for remedies in this world and painted their solutions in terms of cosmic destruction and recreation. More recently, interpreters are plumbing the deep ways in which even proto-apocalyptic texts draw upon earlier prophetic books. This research strengthens the historical and literary connections between prophetic and apocalyptic literature.[5]

At a most basic level, apocalyptic discourse shares with biblical prophecy something like an oracular quality. Like prophets, apocalyptic visionaries receive messages from the divine realm that are otherwise unavailable to mortals. The biblical prophets announce what the LORD has said with a sense of direct authority very much like that of the apocalyptic visionaries. "Thus says the LORD" implies direct access to divine knowledge. Some biblical prophetic books introduce themselves as "visions," whether they contain much visionary material or not (Isa 1:1; Obad 1:1; Nah 1:1). When John addresses his apocalypse to the seven churches of Asia with greetings directly from God and from Jesus Christ (Rev 1:1-4), it sounds very much like Jeremiah (11:1-3) or any other Hebrew prophet.

More commonly interpreters identify proto-apocalyptic passages through their depiction of cosmic chaos and recreation. New Testament passages in the Gospels and in Revelation in particular speak of cosmic portents and tribulation. Compare these passages from Mark and Isaiah.

In those days, after the suffering of that time, the sun will become dark, and the moon won't give its light. The stars will fall from the sky, and the powers and other heavenly bodies will be shaken. Then they will see the Human One coming in the clouds with great power and splendor. (Mark 13:24-26)	On that day, the Lord will punish the forces of heaven in heaven, and the kings of the earth on earth. They will be gathered together like prisoners in a pit, shut into a prison, and punished after many days. The moon will be diminished, and the sun will fade, since the Lord of heavenly forces will rule on Mount Zion and in Jerusalem, glorious before his elders. (Isa 24:21-23)

Let's remember that "proto-apocalyptic" is a category invented by scholars who want to understand apocalyptic literature. No ancient Israelite or Judahite author thought he was composing "proto-apocalyptic" literature. Yet the widely recognized proto-apocalyptic texts all include this feature. Isaiah 24–27 features the earth broken apart and staggering like a drunkard, along with the Lord striking the sea serpent and the sea dragon with a sword, images that resonate deeply in Revelation 12 and 19. Ezekiel 38–39 narrates an enormous battle between God and Israel's enemies, again appropriated in Revelation 16 and 20. Joel, describing an actual plague of locusts, envisions the earth quaking and the sun, moon, and stars darkened (Joel 2:10), while a war in Zechariah pits God against "all the nations" and culminates when God's feet land on the Mount of Olives, causing an earthquake that splits it in two (Zech 14:2-4).

Heavenly interpreters provide one hallmark of the literary apocalypses. Every ancient apocalypse includes a heavenly figure who guides the visionary, often questioning but always interpreting the vision itself. That device appears in the proto-apocalyptic literature as well. Ezekiel's vision of the dry bones features a conversation between the Lord and the prophet, a device hardly unique among the prophets. The distinctive moment occurs when the LORD interprets the vision to Ezekiel: "these bones are the entire house of Israel..." (Ezek 37:11). Zechariah includes several such visions, featuring "the messenger speaking with me," also identified as "the LORD's messenger" (1:7–6:8). Often the prophet asks, "What are these?" provoking the angel's explanation. Ironically, these scenes occur in chapters 1–8, precisely the parts of Zechariah that often are *not* considered proto-apocalyptic. To be sure, similar moments occur in "ordinary" prophetic literature. Jeremiah has conversations with the LORD that include instructions and explanations. (For a classic example, see Jer 13:1-11.) Chapters 7–9 of Amos feature a series of five visions for which the prophet seeks and receives explanations from the LORD. The point is not that heavenly interpreters appear *only* in the apocalypses, but that their appearance represents the development of a device with roots in the prophetic traditions.

In the proto-apocalyptic literature we find not only literary devices but also religious ideas that later crystalize or grow more prominent in the apocalyptic literature. The literary apocalypses often include "tours of heaven," in which a visionary is transported to view heavenly secrets, especially the dwelling places of the dead or of heavenly beings. Sometimes these tours describe imaginary places in great detail, as in Revelation's description of the New Jerusalem. Among other details we learn of the city's twelve gates and twelve foundations, the city's size, and the precious jewels that adorn its walls (Rev 21:10–22:5). That description recalls two other apocalyptic texts from among the Dead Sea Scrolls, Visions of the New Jerusalem and the Temple Scroll from Qumran (identified as 11QTemple), which picture a new holy city and an idealized temple, respectively. Both Revelation's New Jerusalem and these Qumran documents draw inspiration from Ezekiel 40–48. There "a man" guides the prophet in a remarkably detailed exploration of Israel's true house and the land that surrounds it. The most remarkable thing about these accounts, particularly the one in Ezekiel, involves the rich detail accorded to imaginary places. Such visions not only articulate hope for an alternative and blessed future, they also indicate the values according to which such a future is conceivable. The Temple Scroll, for example, sets out the proper garments and sacrificial procedures for the ideal temple.

More controversial is the question of whether the concept of resurrection occurs in Ezekiel's vision of the dry bones (Ezek 37:1-14). The Hebrew

Bible's first clear reference to resurrection occurs in its only apocalypse (Dan 12:1-3). Resurrection entails the dead being restored to life at the end of history. Ezekiel's vision begins with dead bones, which come to life—with flesh and ligaments—upon the prophet's command. As the prophecy continues, it becomes clear that it applies primarily to Israel, which had been scattered first through the Assyrian conquest and then through the Babylonian. In other words, the vision seems to involve the restoration of a people rather than resurrected life for individuals. However, the LORD God then declares: "I'm opening your graves! I will raise you up from your graves, my people, and I will bring you to Israel's fertile land" (Ezek 37:12).

This is a difficult question. Ezekiel's language certainly resembles resurrection language, the idea that those truly dead could be restored to life, but it differs in an important respect. Resurrection implies not only restoration to life but transformation to eternal life. Ezekiel does not seem to imply final transcendence of death, as we find in Daniel 12:1-3. Nevertheless, it is possible that the idea of resurrection shapes the language of Ezekiel at this point.[6]

> **Resurrection versus Immortality**
>
> In worship many Christians recite the Apostles' Creed or some other classic confession of faith. The Apostles' Creed concludes with the confession that one believes "in the resurrection of the body, and the life everlasting." Most people, Christian or otherwise, assume this confession involves the immortality of the soul. When a person dies, it is often thought, her soul leaves her body for its ultimate residence. That's not how the idea of resurrection works, at least not in its most ancient forms.
>
> Not all ancient Jews and Christians believed in a final resurrection. We see this when the Sadducees test Jesus on the topic: this important group of Jewish leaders did not accept the concept (Mark 12:18-27 and parallels). Those who believed in a resurrection expected that people really, truly died, only to be restored to life on the last day. We see this sentiment in John, when Jesus promises to raise up those who come to him "on the last day" (John 6:39-54), and in Paul, who talks about the dead as those who have fallen asleep (e.g., 1 Thess 4:13-18).[7]

Ezekiel reflects another sentiment that would figure prominently in apocalyptic literature, portraying the conflict between good and evil as a battle pitting God against human or supernatural enemies. The portrayal of God as a great warrior has ancient roots. Students of the Hebrew Scriptures are familiar with the Babylonian *Enuma Elish* or the Ugaritic Baal cycle, in which the gods fight for superiority. The narratives of Israel's holy wars often depict Yahweh as a great warrior who fights Israel's battles. So do several psalms (e.g., Psalms 29 and 97). Apocalyptic literature takes on this motif, not only in Revelation when the risen Jesus makes war with the sword of his mouth (Rev 19:15-21) but also in the imagery of the Son of Man riding the clouds (Mark 14:62; Matt 24:30; 26:64; 1 Thess 4:17). Ezekiel 38–39 sketches a great battle in which the mythological Gog and Magog lead an international army against Israel, only to be annihilated by Israel's God. The book of Revelation adapts this motif (Rev 20:8). This literary device takes conflict between nations or groups and projects it onto the cosmos as an ultimate battle between good and evil.

Another concept that makes its way from prophetic to apocalyptic literature involves visions of God's throne. As with the divine warrior motif, the divine throne has ancient roots that include the concept of God as a king surrounded by a court. Several Psalms depict God ruling from the throne (e.g., Pss 9:4, 7; 11:4; 93:2; 97:2). Neither Isaiah 6 nor Ezekiel 1 is normally identified as "proto-apocalyptic," but both passages include visions of the divine throne. Isaiah "sees" the LORD sitting on a throne, surrounded by heavenly beings and smoke (Isa 6:1-11). Ezekiel encounters the throne not in a heavenly court but in "visions of God" (Ezek 1:1). In Ezekiel's vision God's throne resides on a sort of chariot, again accompanied by heavenly beings. The chariot's mobility suggests that God can accompany God's people even into their place of exile. Within Judaism emerged a significant tradition of mysticism, Merkabah or chariot mysticism, in which people sought visions of the divine chariot like Ezekiel's. However, the idea of a divine throne figures prominently in both Jewish and Christian apocalyptic literature, particularly the tours of heaven. A great deal of the action in Revelation revolves around the divine throne.

Beyond the prophetic literature, apocalyptic discourse also resonates deeply with Jewish wisdom literature. Recognition of this phenomenon has waxed and waned among scholars but has gained solid grounding in recent years. We often think of wisdom and apocalyptic discourses as very different. Whereas Jewish wisdom literature emphasizes the orderly, rational workings of the cosmos, apocalyptic discourse portrays a grand conflict between good and evil. Nevertheless, we find apocalyptic concepts and influences among influential wisdom texts. For example, the Wisdom of Solomon includes a judgment scene rich in apocalyptic imagery (Wis 4:20–5:23).[8] Meanwhile, quite a few apocalyptic texts include wisdom themes.[9] To offer one pointed example, the first half of Daniel establishes a conflict between Daniel's wisdom and that of the other "wise men" in the royal court, while Daniel concludes by establishing a special role for "those skilled in wisdom" (Dan 11:33-35; 12:1-10). Daniel's career as an interpreter of dreams recalls that of the biblical patriarch Joseph, who dominates an outsized section of Genesis, chapters 37–48. Interpreters of Genesis have long identified the Joseph cycle's distinctive nature, identifying it as an expression of wisdom literature. The link between the mystical experiences of dreams and visions with prophecy and apocalypticism, a phenomenon some call *mantic wisdom*, can be identified in many cultures.[10] The apocalypses *4 Ezra* and *2 Baruch* ponder the classic wisdom question of how God relates to injustice. And *1 Enoch* devotes heavy attention to the orderly workings of the cosmos, especially in the *Book of the Watchers* (chaps. 1–36).

It is clear that apocalyptic literature interacts with a wide range of cultural influences from the ancient Near East and Mediterranean world. Likewise, apocalyptic literature interacts with Jewish prophetic and wisdom traditions in complicated ways. Rather than seek single lines of influence from one source to another, we usually do better to imagine ancient apocalyptic discourse in terms of creative adaptations of familiar concepts and themes.

First Enoch and Daniel: The First Literary Apocalypses

The first great Jewish apocalypses, *1 Enoch* and Daniel, proved highly influential among both Jews and Christians. Eleven fragmentary manuscripts from *1 Enoch* appear among the Dead Sea Scrolls, and the book clearly influenced other Jewish literature, such as the (also popular) book of *Jubilees* and *Testaments of the Twelve Patriarchs*. The New Testament epistle of Jude cites *1 Enoch* as scripture (Jude 14-15), and other passages in the New Testament bear resemblance to or perhaps depend upon parts of *1 Enoch*.[11] Other books associated with Enoch also appeared, including *2* and *3 Enoch* and the *Book of the Giants*, which is now lost to us. This body of literature suggests a literary and mystical apocalyptic tradition revolving around the figure of Enoch. For its part, Daniel influenced Revelation more heavily than did any other scriptural work, and Daniel's image of the Son of Man (literally, one like a son of man) riding on clouds shapes early Christian portrayals of Jesus's return (Mark 14:62; Matt 24:30; 26:64; 1 Thess 4:17; Rev 1:7). The Christian Apocrypha includes additions to Daniel known as *The Prayer of Azariah*, *Susanna*, and *Bel and the Dragon*. These additions derive from the Septuagint, the Greek translations of the Hebrew Scriptures that were popular among ancient Jews and Christians alike. *First Enoch* and Daniel both attained wide readership and influence, especially within apocalyptic traditions.

Both *1 Enoch* and Daniel have complicated histories of composition. *First Enoch* naturally divides into five constituent books and some additional material (chaps. 106–108). The composition of these various parts may cover four centuries. The *Book of the Watchers* (chaps. 1–36) and the *Astronomical Book* (chaps. 72–82) both derive from the third century BCE. These books show little interest in political history or the end times; instead, they focus upon the revelation of celestial mysteries. The *Book of the Watchers* provides an account for the origins of evil: rebellious angels impregnated mortal women, creating a wild race of giants and wreaking havoc among humankind (see Gen 6:1-4). The book investigates the places of their punishment. Both the *Book of the Watchers* and the *Astronomical Book* show interest in the movements of celestial bodies and the identities of supernatural beings like angels.

Concern with politics and history emerge in the *Dream Visions* (chaps. 83–90) and the *Epistle of Enoch* (chaps. 91–105). Along with Daniel 7–12, these sections are extremely important for the apocalyptic interpretation of empire and history, the kinds of concerns that dominate the book of Revelation.[12] As we saw in chapter 1, the reign of Antiochus IV Epiphanes and the Maccabean Revolt of 167–164 BCE created enormous cultural pressure. The *Dream Visions* and the *Epistle of Enoch* both describe Israel's history to include the overthrow of Antiochus and the inauguration of a new age. So does Daniel 11. This pattern of social crisis, political upheaval, and divine intervention to preserve the righteous proves formative for later apocalyptic literature.

The *Parables of Enoch*, chaps. 37–71, have proven especially controversial for interpreters. This section includes extensive revelation concerning a messianic figure or "Son of Man" who comes to save and judge the world. Also identified as the "Anointed One" (or messiah), "Chosen One," or "Righteous One," this figure seems to reflect further development upon the idea of "one like a son of man" (Dan 7:13, literal translation). Although the imagery of Revelation 1:13-16 clearly draws upon Daniel 7, other early Christian references to the Son of Man more closely resemble the imagery from the *Parables*.[13] As a result, many interpreters date the *Parables* to the first or even the second century CE. Some even regard the book as a Christian work, but most do not. At any rate, the *Parables* reveal development in the concepts of messiah and Son of Man.

Like *1 Enoch*, Daniel may be divided into parts. Curiously, a middle section of Daniel (2:4b–7:28) was composed in Aramaic, with the rest of the book in Hebrew. That linguistic division is significant, but so is another. The book is often remembered for the heroic tales that dominate chapters 1–6. Daniel and his friends reject the king's diet, but God blesses them with extraordinary health. Daniel not only interprets the king's dream, he does so without being told its contents. Shadrach, Meshach, and Abednego refuse to worship the king's statue, but are miraculously delivered from the fiery furnace. Daniel prays to the God of Israel during a period in which prayer may only be directed to King Darius, but God saves Daniel from the lions' den. These familiar stories mark Daniel in popular memory, but the entirety of Daniel 7–12 constitutes the Hebrew Bible's only literary apocalypse. A key question for interpreters involves how to relate Daniel's Hebrew and Aramaic sections and how to relate its legends with its visions.

Some readers—including myself in the past—see the legends and the apocalyptic sections offering basically a consistent message. The apocalyptic sections clearly reflect concern with Antiochus and the Maccabean Revolt. They call the audience to wisdom: a wisdom that requires faithfulness to the emerging distinctives of Judaism along with the rejection of violence. In the end, the book promises, God will destroy Antiochus, inaugurate a new and more "human" rule, and deliver the righteous to eternal blessedness. According to this reading, the legends basically encourage the same outlook: Daniel and his friends refuse to compromise their traditional diet or their fidelity to Israel's God, and God looks after their safety.

More recently, interpreters perceive a change in outlook from one section to the other. Daniel 1–6 imagines that faithful Jews can endure and survive within a context that includes flawed, sometimes dangerous, Gentile kings. In response to Antiochus, and perhaps in response to the violence that marked the Hellenistic period, Daniel 7–12 rejects that premise. God must do away with evil rulers in order for faithful Jews to flourish, with the Jewish people playing a critical role in God's rule over the earth.[14] In this sense Daniel functions as anti-imperial or resistance literature. It reveals Antiochus as murderous and blasphemous, and it offers both hope and advice for those who seek to endure the Revolt. A section of *Enoch* called the *Apocalypse of Weeks* (91:11-17; 93:1-10) calls for the righteous to take up arms, Daniel emphasizes that the wise should pursue "nonviolent resistance and covenant obedience," "a stance of faithful waiting for God to act."[15]

The other division within Daniel involves the blending of Hebrew and Aramaic sections. Oddly, the Aramaic section includes most but not all of the legends but only chapter 7 of the apocalyptic section. This Aramaic section begins with the dream of King Nebuchadnezzar and continues through Daniel's vision of the four beasts. These two units are united by a common theme: a succession of four oppressive empires that must all pass away, followed by a kingdom instituted by God "that will be indestructible" (Dan 2:44; see 7:27). According to Anathea E. Portier-Young, the combination of Aramaic and Hebrew sections functions in a way that reinforces the movement from the legends to the visions: "to move the audience from a posture of partial accommodation and collaboration to one of total rejection of Seleucid hegemony and domination."[16]

The oldest sections of *1 Enoch* use visions to explore great mysteries like the origins of evil and the organization of the cosmos. In response to Antiochus and the crisis he precipitated, the *Dream Visions* and the *Epistle of Enoch* present hope for divine deliverance and a call to revolt. During that same crisis, Daniel too offers a path for resistance, albeit a nonviolent way. *First Enoch* and Daniel, then, open the path to a new form of literature, the literary apocalypse. These books also develop the tour of heavenly mysteries, which Enoch pursues, and they set the precedent for apocalyptic discourse as political resistance.

One more thing about *1 Enoch* and Daniel. Both visionaries, Enoch and Daniel, represent legendary figures. A seventh-generation human, Enoch lives 365 years. More remarkably, he escapes death: "Enoch walked with God and disappeared because God took him" (Gen 5:24). As for Daniel, within the Bible he is known only as a particularly virtuous and wise man and is grouped with Noah and Job (Ezek 14:14, 20; 28:3). Daniel may have carried other legendary associations, but nothing is truly known of him. As visionaries, Enoch and Daniel introduce the technique of *pseudonymity*: all of the Jewish and Christian apocalypses, with the exception of Revelation and the *Shepherd of Hermas*, are attributed to great figures of the past. Many of the visionaries have mystical associations: in some traditions Enoch, Moses, and Baruch have escaped death, while Moses and Isaiah are said to have "seen" God. Pseudonymity is a hallmark of the apocalyptic literary tradition.

The Dead Sea Scrolls

Collectively the Dead Sea Scrolls mark the most significant archaeological discovery in the history of biblical studies. An initial find in 1947 led to the uncovering of thousands of documents and fragments of documents in eleven caves scattered around a site called Qumran (today in the Palestinian territories), along with the excavation of the entire site. The story of this discovery, including the marketing, assembly, translation, and publication of the Scrolls, makes a fascinating tale, complete with cloak-and-dagger exchanges and international intrigue.[17] Written between the second century BCE and the first century CE, the Scrolls include many documents scholars had never encountered before and fairly full texts previously known only in fragments, along with familiar biblical and non-canonical works. The Scrolls are important because they reveal the kinds of concerns some Jews held during a very important period, including (for our purposes) the emergence of both apocalyptic literature and early Christianity.

> **The Dead Sea Scrolls in English**
> Two English translations of the Scrolls are especially popular in classrooms. Geza Vermes, *The Complete Dead Sea Scrolls in English* (7th ed.; Penguin Classics; New York: Penguin, 2012), is the handiest, while Florentino García Martínez, *The Dead Sea Scrolls Translated: The Qumran Texts in English* (2nd ed.; Grand Rapids: Eerdmans, 1996), is slightly more comprehensive.

We cannot know for certain how the Dead Sea Scrolls relate to ancient people and movements. For example, should we think of them as a library that included all kinds of perspectives from all sorts of movements or as the particular library of a movement, including texts that reflect the distinctive views of the community that gathered at Qumran? Nevertheless, it is entirely fair to say that apocalyptic topics and apocalyptic texts are abundant among the Scrolls. *First Enoch* and *Jubilees*, a massive reinterpretation of Genesis and Exodus heavy in apocalyptic content, are well represented among the Scrolls. Some scrolls, like the *Habakkuk Pesher* (1QpHab, a commentary on the book of Habakkuk), interpret biblical texts as predictions of a particular group and its experiences. To many, it looks as if the *Habakkuk Pesher* recounts the history of the Qumran community. Others, like the *Damascus Document* (CD) and the *Community Rule* (1QS), spell out standards for community life and reflect a general apocalyptic outlook. For example, several Qumran documents portray humanity as divided into two camps, the righteous and the wicked, the character of persons determined by God before their birth. Some of the Scrolls speculate concerning the identity and roles of heavenly beings, a few express messianic hope, and many reflect concern regarding the last days.

> **Dead Sea Scroll Shorthand**
> Scholars identify the Scrolls through a sort of shorthand, reflected in the text here. For example, the designation 11QTemple for the *Temple Scroll* indicates Cave 11 at Qumran (11Q), followed by the subject matter of the scroll. Conventions can vary, with some identifying scrolls only by number and others by subject matter (e.g., 11Q15 = 11QHymns).

Beyond texts that reflect an apocalyptic outlook, a few of the Scrolls thoroughly devote themselves to apocalyptic speculation. The *War Rule* (1QM) spells out highly ritualized rules for battle between the Sons of Light and the Sons of Darkness. One would pity the army that would follow such procedures; the *War Rule* counts on divine intervention. Like Ezekiel 40–48 and Revelation 21–22, a few scrolls sketch the plans for an ideal temple and a new Jerusalem. The *Temple Scroll* (11QTemple) provides the most prominent example.

If the Scrolls represent the outlook of the Qumran community to any significant degree, that community held a sharply apocalyptic point of view. If the Scrolls are not so closely tied to the community, they still yield evidence for the emergence of apocalyptic sensibilities beginning in the period of Daniel and parts of *1 Enoch* and continuing into the emergence of Christianity.

Biblical Retellings: *Jubilees* and the *Testaments of the Twelve Patriarchs*

One literary form common among ancient Jews involved the retelling of biblical narratives. This literary genre necessarily involved reinterpretation of the canonical story in order to bring out emphases important to the authors. Some such texts simply retell the familiar narrative with additional details and emphases; others provide expansions that fill out details or narrative gaps from the biblical account. *Jubilees* essentially retells Genesis 1–Exodus 24 with heavily apocalyptic content. With Jewish roots and Christian additions, the *Testaments of the Twelve Patriarchs* imagines the last words the twelve sons of Jacob/Israel *would have said* to their descendants. Sections of the *Testaments* amount to short literary apocalypses.

Probably written in the wake of the Maccabean Revolt, *Jubilees* presents itself as having been narrated by God directly to Moses during Moses's ascent up Mount Sinai to receive the tablets of the law. Like the literary apocalypses, *Jubilees* presents itself as what God "revealed" to Moses, particularly through the "angel of the presence" (*Jub.* 1:4, 29); unlike the literary apocalypses, the revelation is entirely verbal rather than visionary. It begins with a pessimistic outlook: Israel will rebel against God and lose its land, but God will stand beside them and reestablish them. This basic outlook is shared by the biblical prophetic books: Israel has suffered for its unfaithfulness, but God has returned the people to their land and given them a new temple and a new kingdom.

When *Jubilees* recounts the history of creation, of the patriarchs, and of Israel's deliverance from Egypt, readers immediately recognize both the contours of the biblical story and the massive innovations included in *Jubilees*. For example, the creation of the heavens, the earth, and the waters includes an accounting of various heavenly beings (*Jub.* 2:2). The creation of sun, moon, and stars indicates not only night and day but the foundations for Israel's sacred calendar, including feast days, sabbath years, and jubilees (2:9). Regulations concerning the impurity that comes upon women with childbirth (see Lev 12:1-2) are written back into the story of Eve (*Jub.* 3:9-14). When the book recounts the names of the primeval ancestors, Enoch receives special attention as one who learned writing and esoteric knowledge, including a summary of the contents of *1 Enoch* (*Jub.* 4:16-26). In fact, *Jubilees* shares with *1 Enoch* the tradition of the "Watchers" (or rebellious angels) and their punishment as an interpretation of Genesis 6:1-4 (*Jub.* 5:1-11). Into the story of Noah *Jubilees* inserts a divine sanction for the 364-day (solar) calendar rather than a lunar calendar of 360 days, an essential consideration for persons charged with observing holy days and festivals on the correct dates. When Jacob blesses his sons on his deathbed, Genesis 49 shows no awareness that the descendants of Levi will serve as priests, a role not revealed until Numbers 1:49-50; *Jubilees* places the blessing of Levi first and identifies his priestly commission during Jacob's lifetime (*Jub.* 30:18-20; 31:11-17). *Jubilees* blames a sort of Satan figure, Mastema, for Abraham's aborted slaughter of Isaac (*Jub.* 17:15-18) and for hindering Israel's escape from Egypt (48:9-19). *Jubilees* features a revelation concerning the final generation, when Israel will return to God and be delivered from its oppressors and the spirits of the righteous dead will live in joy (*Jub.* 23:11-31). These and countless other examples show that *Jubilees* was written, in part, to address the particular concerns of priestly groups and that *Jubilees* participates heavily in apocalyptic speculation.

True to its name, the *Testaments of the Twelve Patriarchs* narrates a final address by each of Jacob's twelve sons to his descendants. Each testament follows a similar thematic outline. Apocalyptic interests such as a dualistic teaching concerning the two ways persons might follow and the two spirits that guide people; the influence of wicked and righteous angels, including Beliar or Satan; and a final apostasy followed by the restoration of Israel's twelve tribes, resurrection, and judgment pervade the book. Moreover, four mini-apocalypses appear among the testaments, most notably *Testament of Levi* 2–5 (but see also *T.Levi* 8; *T.Naphtali* 6; and *T.Joseph* 19).

Dating the *Testaments* has proven especially controversial. Multiple allusions to *1 Enoch* indicate authors familiar with key parts of that work. They clearly include Christian material such as a virgin giving birth to an unblemished lamb (*T.Joseph* 19) and an allusion to a messiah who receives the Holy Spirit as the heavens open above him (*T.Judah* 24:1-2). Some interpreters attribute the *Testaments* entirely to Christian authorship, a position that would remove their relevance as antecedents for New Testament apocalyptic literature. Most, however, see a second-century CE Christian document that builds upon second-century BCE Jewish material.

How Many Heavens?

Several apocalypses feature tours of heaven, in which the visionary passes through multiple levels of heaven. Paul mentions visiting the third heaven (2 Cor 12:1-10), as does the fourth-century CE *Apocalypse of Paul*. *Third Baruch* mentions five or possibly seven. The *Testament of Levi* has seven, as do *2 Baruch*, the *Apocalypse of Abraham*, and the *Ascension of Isaiah*. One passage in *2 Enoch* (20:3) mentions ten heavens. The concept of multiple heavens emerges fairly late in apocalyptic literature, no earlier than the first century CE.[18]

The longer apocalypse in the *Testament of Levi* 2–5 opens as a classic literary apocalypse. Levi enters a state of spiritual reflection, then falls asleep. The heavens open for him, and a voice calls him to enter. Levi explores seven heavens as an angelic interpreter explains what he sees. Levi learns of a period of terrible judgment upon humanity as well as punishments against evil spirits. Evil persons will not repent but persist in their ways despite their torment—a pattern we encounter in Revelation. Ultimately Levi visits the throne room of God. The *Testament of Levi* includes messianic hope in language that suggests Christian authorship (*T.Levi* 2:11), but it includes other material that seems to focus upon Israel without Christian interest.

Jewish Apocalypses in the First Century CE

We close this survey of Jewish apocalyptic literature with two great literary apocalypses that clearly overlap the emergence of Christianity. Probably composed very near the writing of Revelation, *4 Ezra* and *2 Baruch* constitute the most influential of the Jewish apocalypses from the period. (*Third Baruch* and the *Apocalypse of Abraham* are also significant.)

Both *4 Ezra* and *2 Baruch* reflect upon the fall of Jerusalem in 70 CE, treating it not only as a tragedy but as a theological and religious problem. The two books refer to the fall of Jerusalem to "Babylon," an allusion to the destruction of Jerusalem and its first temple in 587/586 BCE. They also adopt pseudonymous visionaries, Ezra and Baruch, who are associated with Jerusalem's fall to the Babylonians: Baruch the scribe of Jeremiah is exiled to Egypt prior to the catastrophe; after the Persians returned some of the exiles from Babylon to Yehud (later, Judea), the king commissions Ezra to reconstitute Jerusalem's society. Both *4 Ezra* and *2 Baruch* interpret the sacking of Jerusalem by Rome as analogous to its fall to the Babylonians.

Following the standard biblical interpretation of national suffering, these books assume that Jews somehow contributed to their own demise. But it is not as if Jews in Judea and Galilee were somehow "worse" than the Romans who dominated them. Why would God allow an oppressive and exploitative empire to decimate God's own city and its people? What is God's role in such calamity? And how should God's people respond to a crisis such as this?

Fourth Ezra, which occurs as chapters 3–14 of 2 Esdras in the Apocrypha, addresses these questions through a series of seven dialogues and visions. In the first three visions Ezra presses hard questions against God and the angel Uriel.

> I answered, "I beg you, Lord, why has the sense of understanding been given to me? It wasn't my purpose to ask about the ways above but about the things that we see every day. Why has Israel been handed over to the Gentiles to our shame? Why has the people you loved been given over to godless tribes? Why has the Law of our ancestors been invalidated and the written ordinances come to nothing? Why do we pass from the world like locusts and our life like a mist? Why aren't we worthy to obtain mercy? What will God do for the sake of his name, which is bestowed on us? About these things I have asked." (*4 Ezra* 4:22-25)

Ezra is plagued by his failure to understand God's apparent abandonment of Jerusalem, not only for the people's sake but in terms of God's own reputation. "It would have been better not to have come into being than to come here, live in the middle of wickedness, suffer, and not understand why" (*4 Ezra* 4:12). Remarkably, Ezra receives a series of answers that fail to satisfy him. Instead, the book's fourth vision (*4 Ezra* 9:26–10:59) transforms his perspective. Ezra scolds a woman for grieving the death of her only son: after all, what is her individual suffering in comparison to that of Jerusalem? She undergoes a terrifying transformation that ultimately reveals her as a gloriously restored new Jerusalem. Somehow this religious experience transforms Ezra: he not only ceases scolding the woman, he also abandons his challenges and becomes receptive to the forthcoming visions.

The fifth vision of *4 Ezra* somewhat recalls Daniel's vision of the four beasts and the one like a son of man; in fact, the passage links itself directly to Daniel's fourth beast (*4 Ezra* 11:39-40). In some ways the fifth vision also resembles the account of the Beast of Revelation 13. Ezra sees an eagle, a primary symbol of Roman imperial power, that flew "to rule over the earth and over those who lived on the earth" (*4 Ezra* 11:5) while oppressing the poor and committing violence against the peaceable (11:41-42).

A lion (see Rev 5:5) pronounces the eagle's doom. We then learn that the lion represents the messiah, who will judge the wicked and free the righteous at the end of days (*4 Ezra* 12:31-34). The book's sixth vision provides another messianic image, a man who rises out of the sea to ride with the clouds of heaven (*4 Ezra* 13:2-4). An "innumerable multitude" gathers for war against this messiah, who destroys his enemies with fire and gathers a peaceable people (*4 Ezra* 13:5-13). The vision even identifies this man from the sea as God's "Son" (13:32, 52), who rebuilds Zion, judges the wicked, gathers Israel's "lost" tribes, and inaugurates a blessed new age.

Fourth Ezra's seventh vision is fascinating in that Ezra is commissioned to dictate ninety-four books, the public and canonical twenty-four books of the Hebrew Bible plus seventy books reserved for the wise (*4 Ezra* 14:45-47). More important, however, is the advice Ezra delivers to the people. The vision echoes the call of Moses, with a voice calling Ezra from a bush. The voice reminds Ezra of Moses's commission to deliver the Torah, but it also reveals that Moses received secret knowledge concerning the end times (*4 Ezra* 14:1-6). We remember that Ezra is credited with rediscovering and restoring the very Torah Moses passed down. As Moses did, Ezra gathers the people, reminds them that they have transgressed the "law of life," and promises that if they discipline themselves in righteous ways they will obtain mercy after death (*4 Ezra* 14:27-35). In the end, *4 Ezra* promises a messiah who will restore Israel's glory and afterlife hope for those who follow the ways of Torah. The apocalypse begins with Ezra's critical questions, but it concludes with a call to obedience.

Second Baruch asks similar questions to those posed in *4 Ezra*. Like *4 Ezra*, *2 Baruch* demonstrates the visionary's reluctance to look upon Jerusalem's devastation and his desire for understanding. Both books feature dialogue between the visionary and God and other heavenly beings, although *2 Baruch* relies less heavily upon vision reports. However, *2 Baruch* stands apart in three primary ways: in comparison with Ezra, Baruch tends to accept the answers he receives without challenging them; he addresses the general population more extensively; and his revelations provide more specific pictures of the end times.

When Baruch asks what lies in the future and how God's name will be glorified (*2 Bar.* 3:1-9), concerns *4 Ezra* shares, he learns that Zion's devastation is only temporary and a future Zion is yet to be revealed (4:1-7). When Baruch suggests that Zion's fall will injure God's reputation for protecting Israel (*2 Bar.* 5:1), he learns that God's glory is eternal while God's judgment must occur in its own time (5:2-4). When he complains, as Ezra does, that the even more wicked Babylon fares better than Zion (*2 Bar.* 11:1-3), he finds that God is impartial but judges Israel in order to redeem and forgive it (13:5-12). When he wonders why people should pursue righteous, given the apparent lack of reward for faithfulness (*2 Bar.* 14:4-7), the answer lies in the world to come (15:1-8). For whatever Baruch asks, there's an answer that satisfies him.[19]

The specific eschatological teachings of *2 Baruch* occur in a series of twelve tribulations (chap. 27), and in the visions of the forest, vine, fountain, and cedar (chaps. 36–40) and of the cloud (chaps. 53–74). The visions are all unique, and their teachings do not necessarily cohere. Like other apocalypses, *2 Baruch* sees a time of great distress before ultimate vindication arrives. At the end of the twelve calamities arrives the Anointed One (or messiah), who will inaugurate an age of miraculous plenty followed by a resurrection of the righteous (chaps. 28–30). The forest, vine, fountain, and cedar images recapitulate the familiar theme of four empires, with the messiah finally killing the leader of the fourth empire and establishing his rule. Through a vision of a cloud containing a series of twelve black and white waters, *2 Baruch* reviews the entire history of Israel through the Babylonian conquest. At the end of the series comes the messiah who destroys Israel's enemies and brings about the blessed messianic age.

Second Baruch also includes three major speeches to the people, which demonstrate how people should respond to the vision (chaps. 31–34; 44–46; 77–87). The first two speeches address the people of Jerusalem; the third is an epistle to the exiles in Babylon. Baruch interprets Jerusalem's fall as God's judgment upon the people, and he calls for obedience to the Torah as the remedy—as does *4 Ezra*. Indeed, all three speeches call for loyalty to the law. The people are to seek salvation not in leaders, who fail and perish, but in the eternal law (*2 Bar.* 77:13-16).

Written in the wake of Jerusalem's devastation, *4 Ezra* and *2 Baruch* pose challenging questions concerning God's faithfulness toward Israel. In the end, both apocalypses promise a messiah who will annihilate Israel's oppressors and inaugurate a blessed new age for the elect. *Second Baruch* even extends hope for Gentiles who follow the right path (*2 Bar.* 42:5). Both apocalypses also express resurrection hope. Perhaps most importantly, both apocalypses propose observing the Torah as the path to salvation.

Conclusion

Because this book is devoted to New Testament apocalyptic literature, we have treated biblical and Jewish apocalyptic discourse as a "background" to the New Testament. That's unfortunate, because the texts we have discussed in this chapter are interesting in their own right and have literary and religious integrity of their own. Readers who study these texts independently will find an abundance of fascinating material. For example, sections of *1 Enoch* like the *Astronomical Book* reflect the sort of speculation that marks ancient science: without modern scientific resources, how did people account for the cosmos and its workings? I have often asked students to read these sections of *1 Enoch* alongside popular Greek philosophical texts that also discuss natural philosophy. Daniel and *1 Enoch's Dream Visions* indicate conflicting responses to a political and religious crisis, with Daniel recommending nonviolence and the *Dream Visions* celebrating revolt. *Fourth Ezra* includes some of the most compelling reflections concerning God's responsibility for human evil we will find anywhere—and its questions never achieve resolution. Diverse in literary form, social attitudes, and religious outlook, the apocalyptic literature of ancient Judaism has a great deal to offer contemporary readers.

In treating ancient Jewish literature as "background" we also obscure an essential reality: very little of the New Testament is "Christian" as distinct from "Jewish." Some historians refuse to apply the term "Christian" to those groups because the concept of a religion called "Christianity" did not form until after the New Testament period. The few occurrences of the word "Christian" in the New Testament refer not to a religion, much less the Christians' own self-designation, but to an accusation from outsiders: the "Christians" were messianists (that's what "Christian" means) who followed a failed revolutionary. The New Testament's "Christian" references all occur in contexts of accusation, trial, or persecution (Acts 11:26; 26:28; 1 Pet 4:16). On the other hand, the people who followed and venerated Jesus formed a distinctive movement with its own diversity and coherence. They formed churches rather than synagogues, they experienced conflict with synagogues, and one very important leader within the movement, Paul, speaks of being "in Christ." Hence, the boundaries between "Jewish" and "Christian" literature are fuzzy at best. Early Christians did not regard biblical and noncanonical literature as "Jewish." Jewish and Gentile devotees of Jesus alike considered those writings their own and treated them as such.

At the same time, New Testament apocalyptic discourse did not emerge in a cultural vacuum. As I too often remind my students—I ask them to say it along with me—Jesus was Jewish, Peter was Jewish, Paul was Jewish, Mary Magdalene was Jewish, and so on. The apocalyptic concepts and literary devices we encounter in New Testament and other early Christian literature all draw upon the innovations that created and adapted apocalyptic traditions in ancient Judaism.

For Further Reading

Beyerle, Stefan. "The Imagined World of the Apocalypses." Pages 373–87 in *The Oxford Handbook of Apocalyptic Literature*. Edited by John J. Collins. New York: Oxford University Press, 2014.

Bremmer, Jan N. "Descents to Hell and Ascents to Heaven in Apocalyptic Literature." Pages 340–57 in *The Oxford Handbook of Apocalyptic Literature*. Edited by John J. Collins. New York: Oxford University Press, 2014.

Carey, Greg. *Ultimate Things: An Introduction to Jewish and Christian Apocalyptic Literature*. St. Louis: Chalice Press, 2005.

Collins, John J. *The Apocalyptic Imagination: An Introduction to Jewish Apocalyptic Literature.* 2nd ed. Grand Rapids: Eerdmans, 1998.

Cook, Stephen L. "Apocalyptic Prophecy." Pages 19–35 in in *The Oxford Handbook of Apocalyptic Literature.* Edited by John J. Collins. New York: Oxford University Press, 2014.

———. *Prophecy and Apocalypticism: The Postexilic Social Setting.* Minneapolis: Fortress Press, 1995.

deSilva, David A. *The Jewish Teachers of Jesus, James, and Jude: What Earliest Christianity Learned from the Apocrypha and Pseudepigrapha.* New York: Oxford University Press, 2012.

Goff, Matthew. "*1 Enoch.*" Pages 224–37 in *The Oxford Encyclopedia of the Books of the Bible,* volume 1. Edited by Michael D. Coogan. New York: Oxford University Press, 2011.

Grabbe, Lester L. "Prophetic and Apocalyptic: Time for New Definitions—and New Thinking." Pages 107–33 in *Knowing the End from the Beginning: The Prophetic, the Apocalyptic, and Their Relationships.* Edited by Lester L. Grabbe and Robert D. Haak. JSPS 46. New York: T and T Clark, 2003.

Himmelfarb, Martha. *Tours of Hell: An Apocalyptic Form in Jewish and Christian Literature.* Philadelphia: Fortress Press, 1983.

Levenson, Jon D. *Resurrection and the Restoration of Israel: The Ultimate Victory of the God of Life.* New Haven, CT: Yale University Press, 2006.

Newsom, Carol A. *Daniel.* Old Testament Library. Louisville: Westminster John Knox Press, 2014.

Portier-Young, Anathea E. *Apocalypse Against Empire: Theologies of Resistance in Early Judaism.* Grand Rapids: Eerdmans, 2011.

Segal, Alan. *Death and the Afterlife: A History of the Afterlife in Western Religion.* New York: Doubleday, 2004.

Sweeney, Marvin A. *Form and Intertextuality in Prophetic and Apocalyptic Literature.* FAT 45. Tübingen: Mohr Siebeck, 2005.

VanderKam, James C. *The Dead Sea Scrolls Today.* 2nd ed. Grand Rapids: Eerdmans, 2010.

Wright, Benjamin G., III, and Lawrence M. Wills, eds. *Conflicted Boundaries in Wisdom and Apocalypticism.* SBLSymS 35. Atlanta: Society of Biblical Literature, 2005.

Chapter Three
The Pauline Epistles

Some readers may wonder why we begin our survey of New Testament apocalyptic literature with Paul rather than with Jesus or with the Gospels. After all, the New Testament canon begins with the four Gospels, not with Paul's letters. More to the point, the Gospels narrate the career of Jesus; Paul's letters were composed twenty or more years after Jesus's career. Does not Jesus represent the starting point for Paul's journey?

These objections all make sense. But we also have good reasons to begin with Paul.

First, Paul likely provides our closest historical witness to Jesus's ministry and the emergence of the movement he inspired. Although the Gospels reflect decades of development and interpretation regarding the shared memories concerning Jesus, Paul himself encountered the Jesus movement within just two to (at most) four years of Jesus's death. We derive this impression from both Acts, in which Paul encounters the risen Jesus on his way to Damascus, and Galatians 1:15–2:1.[1] It is possible that the New Testament epistles of James and Jude were actually composed by Jesus's brothers James and Jude, who would have been Paul's contemporaries, but the majority of interpreters judge both letters to be the products of other authors writing in later decades. In other words, not only do Paul's letters reflect our earliest Christian literature, Paul himself encountered the Jesus movement very close to its beginnings.

Second, Paul represents a response to the Jesus movement from a well-informed Jewish contemporary. Paul represents one of no more than three

Jews from his own period who provide anything resembling a spiritual autobiography,[2] the only Pharisee whose writing survives, and the only first-century Jew who chronicles his own mystical experience.[3] In short, Paul provides a crucial source for historians of first-century Judaism. We cannot know for certain whether Paul had come across Jesus in person, but Paul resisted the messianist movement from its very beginning. We learn this not only from Acts but from Paul's own account. We can speculate as to Paul's motives for persecuting these early Jesus-believers, just as we wonder why Paul himself was persecuted by other Jews. One possibility, however, is that under Roman domination Jewish communities could not tolerate the suspicion associated with the movement's apocalypticism—that is, its proclamation concerning the resurrection, return, and future reign of a crucified seditionist.[4]

These first two justifications for starting with Paul open the path for a third. If we take Paul's apocalypticism seriously as a witness to the first generation of Jesus's followers—at least, to one strand of them—we may have a better background for understanding that movement and its founder. Over the past thirty years or so historians have debated whether or not Jesus was apocalyptically inclined. The earlier consensus had been that, yes, Jesus was an apocalyptic prophet of one kind or another: he proclaimed the imminent arrival of God's kingdom, accompanied by a final judgment. However, the growing body of scholarship on the Gospel of Thomas, discovered only in 1945, revealed a form of Jesus devotion that rejected apocalyptic speculation outright. (We discuss Thomas in chapter 5.) Historians wondered whether Thomas might reflect first-generation memories of Jesus. Some have also observed weaker interest in apocalypticism in other early Christian sources such as James and presumed early layers of Q. These considerations lead many to question the apocalyptic Jesus consensus. Paul, however, represents a follower of Jesus who was familiar with the Jesus movement from its very beginnings and who interpreted Jesus in apocalyptic terms.[5] We might ask how to locate Jesus between John the Baptist, with whom he associated, and Paul, the earliest witness to the Jesus movement. If John the Baptist preached God's imminent intervention in history, and if Paul did as well, perhaps Jesus was himself apocalyptically inclined.

> **Q and the Non-Apocalyptic Jesus**
>
> Most, but not all, scholars believe the authors of Matthew and Luke each relied on two literary sources, the Gospel of Mark and a hypothetical source, now lost to us, we call Q. According to this model, Q constitutes that material that is common to Matthew and Luke but not shared by Mark—about 225–250 verses. Like Thomas, Q would largely amount to a collection of Jesus's sayings.
>
> According to some proposals, Q emerged from a process of composition. Some interpreters claim that apocalyptic concerns are absent from the earliest layers of Q,[6] but other scholars contradict this proposal.[7]

Locating Paul

Paul's influence over later Christian belief guarantees his status as a controversial figure. Of the twenty-seven New Testament documents, thirteen claim Paul as their author. In addition, Paul dominates the second half of Acts, 2 Peter acknowledges the importance of his letters (2 Pet 3:15-16), James may or may not constitute a critical response to Paul's preaching, and Revelation adapts his distinctive epistolary greeting (Rev 1:4-6). Written only a generation of so after Paul's death, the epistle *1 Clement* alludes to Paul's past ministry in Corinth and offers some commentary on 1 Corinthians. Later texts like the *Acts of Paul and Thecla*, the epistles *3 Corinthians* and *Laodiceans*, a fictional correspondence between Paul and the Roman philosopher Seneca, and the *Apocalypse of Paul* demonstrate that Christians continued to write about Paul's life and to write in his name well after his death. A reappraisal of Paul's teaching fueled the Protestant Reformation, and interpreters continue to debate the significance of his message. Modern debates concerning gender relations, slavery, and sexuality frequently revolve around key passages attributed to Paul. For all these reasons, it will prove helpful to step back and consider some basic questions about the apostle before we assess his letters as apocalyptic literature.

An Apostle and Letter Writer

We know Paul best through the letters attributed to him within the New Testament. Yet some critical questions attend how we interpret these letters, and Paul himself, on many matters. Apocalyptic discourse stands as one of those concerns.

The first question involves our sources for interpreting Paul. To be concise, seven letters constitute the most reliable sources for interpreting Paul: Romans, 1 and 2 Corinthians, Galatians, Philippians, 1 Thessalonians, and Philemon. The other possible sources all face serious challenges or complications.

For example, many interpreters rely on Acts to provide a basic chronology of Paul's ministry, but most are skeptical that Acts sketches an accurate picture of Paul's teaching. Simply, one could read Paul's speeches from Acts and wonder if that Paul had ever met the guy who wrote the epistles. Apart from the proclamation of Jesus, there's hardly any overlap between Acts's speeches and Paul's letters.

As for the other six letters composed in Paul's name—Ephesians, Colossians, 2 Thessalonians, 1 and 2 Timothy, and Titus—many scholars consider them pseudonymous, or forged. Majorities of interpreters doubt Paul wrote any of these "disputed" epistles, with opinion more evenly divided for Ephesians, Colossians, and 2 Thessalonians than for 1 and 2 Timothy and Titus. There are many reasons for these judgments, mainly involving the letters' content and literary style. Because so many regard these epistles as pseudonymous, interpreters focus primarily on the "undisputed" epistles, with occasional appeals to the disputed ones. The question of authorship bears especially strongly upon apocalyptic studies. As we shall see below, many interpreters perceive significant differences between undisputed letters like 1 Corinthians and some of the disputed epistles on matters related to apocalyptic eschatology.

Other sources provide still less help. Possible allusions to Paul in 2 Peter, James, and Revelation yield little information at best. The same applies to *1 Clement* and other ancient texts that allude to Paul. The *Acts of Paul and Thecla* tells us more about second-century appropriations of Paul than about Paul himself.

We also take seriously the nature of Paul's letters. Almost all letters are *occasional,* meaning they are written in specific moments for particular audiences and purposes. Paul's are no exception. In other words, Paul composed his epistles in response to the circumstances of particular groups of people who lived in diverse settings. The occasional nature of Paul's letters means that Paul never composed a textbook or manual of his overall thoughts. When we read his letters, we must ask ourselves what problem Paul was speaking to and what he was hoping to accomplish, a process of educated guesswork. At some points Paul may appear to contradict himself: we might explain these differences by appealing to the circumstances and aims of a particular letter or by imagining change and development in Paul's thought.

A Pharisee

In one autobiographical sketch, Paul describes himself as a Pharisee so far as Israel's Law was concerned (Phil 3:5; see Acts 23:6; 26:5). Although some interpreters debate whether or not Paul was in fact a Pharisee, this self-identification lets us know just a little bit about Paul's pre-Jesus belief system. For one thing, the Pharisees believed in the resurrection, a belief that reflects some degree of influence from apocalyptic discourse. Not all Jews believed in the resurrection, but perhaps most did.[8] We'd love to have opinion-poll results from the period, but none have survived. The Pharisees, like the Essenes at Qumran and like Jesus and Paul, believed in the resurrection, while the Sadducees did not.

Acts 23:6-10 dramatizes this division among informed Jews. On trial before the Jerusalem Council, or Sanhedrin, Paul perceives a mixed audience of Pharisees and Sadducees. Choosing the divide-and-conquer strategy, Paul claims both his Pharisaic identity and his resurrection belief. "Brothers, I'm a Pharisee and a descendant of Pharisees. I am on trial because of my hope in the resurrection of the dead" (Acts 23:6). We cannot know how much history lies behind this story, if any, but immediately the

Sadducees and the Pharisees line up in opposition to one another. "Some Pharisees who were legal experts" defend Paul, but the conflict heats up to the point that the tribune seizes Paul and removes him from the scene for his own safety.

In the middle of the story Acts provides this brief characterization of the Pharisees, a portrait roughly confirmed in other sources from the period.[9] While the Sadducees deny the resurrection, along with belief in an angel or a spirit, the Pharisees subscribe to all three doctrines (Acts 23:8). Initially we wonder what belief in an angel or a spirit might mean, but the story suggests an answer. (The explanation I provide here is not particularly common among scholars, but I think it makes good sense of the passage.) The Pharisees' scribes defend Paul by asking, "What if a spirit or angel has spoken to him?" (Acts 23:9). In other words, Acts appears to portray the Pharisees as believing in both the resurrection (something the Jewish historian Josephus confirms) and in revelations mediated by supernatural agents. *If* this is an accurate interpretation of Acts 23:8-9, *if* Acts provides an accurate account of the Pharisees, and *if* Paul indeed participated in the movement, then Paul's Pharisaic background included immersion in apocalyptic thinking.

An Apocalyptic Visionary

Paul devotes only a little attention to his own experience as the recipient of apocalyptic revelations, but he does so at important moments. Paul also acknowledges that other believers undergo revelatory experiences, or apocalypses (1 Cor 14:5-6, 26), but here we focus on Paul's appeals to his own revelations. In both Galatians and 2 Corinthians Paul faces competition from other Christian preachers. In each case he asserts his own mystical experiences—he uses the Greek word *apokalypsis* to describe them.

In 2 Corinthians Paul confronts a group he calls "super-apostles" (2 Cor 11:5). He portrays his opponents as skilled orators who receive payment for their ministry (2 Cor 11:1-15). Paul calls them "false apostles," even Satan's servants—though he refrains from expressing that last insult explicitly (11:12-15). Compared with apparently superior opponents, Paul deftly frames his own side of the rivalry as nothing more than foolishness. He does so when he trains his attention on these opponents (2 Cor 11:1) and when he begins to conclude the discussion (12:11)—as well as throughout the section. Paul also faces the problem that he has undermined his own integrity. Having promised to visit the church in Corinth during a season of controversy, he had changed his plans (2 Cor 1:15–2:4). He denies taking his earlier plans lightly ("vacillating," 1:17 NRSV). As he contemplates a third visit, he knows it may not go smoothly (2 Cor 12:14–13:10).

Under the microscope, as it were, Paul appeals to "visions and revelations from the Lord" as he takes on these "super-apostles" (2 Cor 12:1-10). It seems ancient persons did not draw fine boundaries between visions and revelations: Paul here relates his own mystical experiences as a means of asserting his spiritual authority. He begins vaguely: "I know" a person who was taken up to the third heaven fourteen years ago, he claims. Eventually the passage reveals that Paul is describing his own revelation.

Paul reveals little of the nature of his vision. He cannot relate whether it was an embodied experience or not—and we might wonder what an embodied tour of the third heaven might mean. He does identify this third heaven as "Paradise," a Persian concept that attracted significant attention in Jewish and Christian apocalyptic literature.[10] Paradise imagery involves a lovely garden, full of delights.[11] Luke and Revelation refer to Paradise as a place where the redeemed dwell beyond this life (Luke 23:43; Rev 2:7). Furthermore, Paul relates having "heard unspeakable words that were things no one is allowed to repeat." Such "reserved knowledge," received by the visionary but kept from the audience, occurs in multiple apocalypses (e.g., Rev 10:4; *4 Ezra* 14:45-48).

Whatever the *nature* of Paul's revelation, its *function* is fairly clear. Paul is vying for status. Not only does Paul identify his opponents as false apostles and Satan's messengers (2 Cor 11:13-15), he invokes language he deploys elsewhere just once—when he appeals to his revelatory experiences to combat competing preachers in Galatians. Here Paul admonishes the Corinthians for submitting to "another Jesus" and a "different gospel" (11:4; see Gal 1:6-9). Paul sees no room for compromise or accommodation in this conflict.

Before we move on to Galatians, we might observe how Paul wraps his extraordinary visions in a soft blanket of humility. His appeals amount to "foolishness" (11:1, 16-23; 12:11). To temper his "outstanding revelations," he is given (by God?) a thorn in the flesh. He prays for deliverance from this mysterious ailment, but instead he learns that God's power works through weakness rather than apparent strength (2 Cor 12:6-10). Paul aims even this expression of humility as a dart against his so-impressive enemies: authentic leadership manifests itself through faithfulness in the midst of hardship. This balance of self-assertion and humility constitutes a standard move in Greco-Roman rhetoric, the tradition that trained young men for public speaking. It also functions as a common device in the narration of apocalyptic visions. Visionaries insist upon their unique privilege in receiving revelations, but they also describe their own fears, their limitations, and their solidarity with their audiences.[12]

In Galatians Paul faces a different challenge, and he appeals to a very different set of revelations. Here the challenge involves preachers who would require Gentile converts to convert to Judaism, particularly through the circumcision of male believers. Once again Paul deploys the language of "another gospel" (Gal 1:6), a gospel opposed to the one he proclaims (1:8-9). Paul exceeds the harsh polemic of 2 Corinthians to claim that these opponents "want to pervert the gospel of Christ" (Gal 1:7 NRSV), and he calls down a curse upon them (1:8-9). Drawing on the circumcision imagery, Paul even wishes they would chop themselves off (5:12). We're talking about circumcision, remember?

Once again we find Paul appealing to his apocalypses to buttress his own authority. But this time the visions are different. He makes three claims, and it's less than clear how they relate to one another. It helps to take these claims out of sequence in order to understand how they hold together.

First, Paul provides a bit of autobiography (1:11–2:14), in which he claims that "God had set me apart from birth and called me through his grace. He was pleased to *reveal* his Son to me" (or "in me"; Gal 1:15-16, emphasis added). Here Paul seems to mean something like the story of his vision and so-called conversion narrated in Acts 9. On his way to

Damascus Paul encounters the risen Jesus as a flash of light temporarily blinds him. This encounter transforms Paul into a follower of Jesus and leads the way to his ministry as a preacher of the gospel.

Paul has already asserted that his gospel comes directly from God, not even from other Christian teachers. "It came through a *revelation* of Jesus Christ" (Gal 1:12, emphasis added). Many, perhaps most, interpreters also link this claim to the narrative from Acts 9. If that's what Paul means, his apocalypse reveals the person *of* Christ himself. But this interpretation fails to explain how, exactly, that revelation provides the content for Paul's gospel. Another possibility is that Paul means he received his gospel by means of a revelation *from* Christ. Whether Paul means a revelation *of* or a revelation *from* Jesus, and those options are not mutually exclusive, the basic claim is the same: Paul's gospel comes directly from God, not from human authority.

Finally, Paul describes a significant meeting that involved himself, Barnabas, and Titus on the one hand and the leaders of the Jerusalem church on the other (Gal 2:1-10). The passage appears to provide Paul's account of the meeting described in Acts 15. In Galatians the issue of Paul's authority again stands foremost. He insists that his ministry is at least equivalent to that of the "pillars" in the Jerusalem church: James, Cephas (or Peter), and John. But here Paul claims a different kind of apocalypse: he made the trip to Jerusalem "because of a revelation" (Gal 2:2). In other words, Paul did not visit the Jerusalem leaders because he was summoned or even appointed (see Acts 15:2); he visited because his revelation so guided him.

Paul appeals to a diverse set of revelations. Scholars will debate how these apocalypses relate to one another, but they all occur in contexts of fierce controversy, when Paul pits his authority against "different" gospels and "false" teachers. Moreover, his apocalypses may range from a revelatory encounter with Jesus's person, to a visit into the top tier of heaven, to guidance to behave in very specific ways.

Apocalyptic Topics

Several apocalyptic topics play key roles in Paul's letters. We especially benefit by noticing that Paul appeals to these topics strategically. Some letters draw more heavily on a given set of topics than others do. For example, Paul dwells explicitly on the bodily nature of the resurrection in 1 Corinthians, a topic he never mentions explicitly in, say, Romans or Galatians.

We begin by observing that Paul articulates his basic message, or *gospel*, in fundamentally apocalyptic categories. Many interpreters regard 1 Thessalonians 1:9-10 as the best clue to Paul's core proclamation. First Thessalonians is likely the earliest of Paul's extant letters. Paul recalls at length his initial visit to Thessalonica. Along the way he reminisces about how the Thessalonians received his ministry and his message.

> People tell us about what sort of welcome we had from you and how you turned to God from idols. As a result you are serving the living and true God, and you are waiting for his Son from heaven. His Son is Jesus, who is the one he raised from the dead and who is the one who will rescue us from the coming wrath. (1 Thess 1:9-10)

Paul begins with language any Jew might apply to Gentile converts, or proselytes: they have turned to the living God from idols. But the next three items are thoroughly apocalyptic. The new believers came to (a) wait for Jesus's return, or *parousia*, (b) believe in Jesus's resurrection, and (c) anticipate deliverance from a coming cosmic crisis.

Quite often Paul strategically deploys the pattern of *resurrection, parousia*, and *consummation*, appealing to these topics on the way to making other points. Paul does put these ideas to such use, but they, along with Jesus's crucifixion, also represent the core of his message. In fact, Paul interprets the crucifixion apocalyptically as well: cross and resurrection together define the experience of believers. Through the cross believers have been transferred from one realm of existence into a "new creation" (Gal 6:14-15; see Gal 2:19-20; Rom 6:4-5). These apocalyptic topics—cross, resurrection, *parousia*, and consummation—provide the core from which Paul reasons his way through many problematic situations.

In 1 Corinthians Paul gives the impression that his gospel revolves only around the cross: "I had made up my mind not to think about anything while I was with you except Jesus Christ, and to preach him as crucified" (1 Cor 2:2). However, this impression is tempered by two considerations. First, in 1 Corinthians 1–2 Paul is making a rhetorical point. Some among the Corinthians are basking in their wisdom and spiritual attainment. Paul wants to value service and faithfulness above status and knowledge; indeed, this theme provides the major argument that runs through 1 Corinthians. The cross—God's Son executed in a public and scandalous way (1 Cor 1:23—Paul uses the Greek word *skandalon*)—provides a perfect counterpoint to those who would elevate themselves above others. In other words, perhaps 1 Corinthians 2:2 does not represent an exclusive or categorical statement of Paul's preaching. Indeed, in this same passage Paul invokes an apocalyptic perspective:

> But we speak God's wisdom, secret and hidden, which God decreed before the ages for our glory. None of the rulers of this age understood this; for if they had, they would not have crucified the Lord of glory. (1 Cor 2:7-8 NRSV)

Here Paul portrays Jesus's crucifixion as part of an apocalyptic scenario. It reveals God's "secret" and "hidden" design, a plan that leads to an ultimate glory. The "rulers of this age" (as opposed to the coming age) could not perceive this deep wisdom.[13]

A second consideration takes account of how Paul appeals to the resurrection and return of Jesus throughout the letter. Just a few high points will reveal how important these topics are to Paul's argument. Paul always begins his letters by hinting toward the letter's larger argument. In 1 Corinthians Paul praises God for the spiritual gifts with which the Corinthians are "made rich" (1 Cor 1:6). They "aren't missing any spiritual gift." But then Paul adds the qualifier: "while you wait for our Lord Jesus Christ to be revealed" (1:7). Moreover, Christ will strengthen and protect the Corinthians "on the day of our Lord Jesus Christ" (1 Cor 1:8). Remarkably, Paul concludes the body of the letter by returning to precisely this point. Chapter 16 amounts to closing important business, but Paul devotes chapter 15 entirely to the resurrection and return of Jesus—the longest discussion of the resurrection in all his letters. (Paul did not write with chapters and verses. Here we simply refer to them to indicate large blocks of material.)

How central is Jesus's return in Paul's thought? It even shapes his thoughts on human sexuality. Paul doesn't offer much advice concerning sexual expression. Apart from warning men to avoid adultery (1 Thess 4:1-8) and prostitution (1 Cor 6:12-20), he doesn't say much. He disapproves of sex between a man and his father's "woman" (1 Cor 5:1-13). Modern church debates concerning sexual ethics often lock in on Paul's brief discussion of same-sex sex in Romans 1:26-27; even there he offers no actual moral instruction. But in 1 Corinthians 7 Paul launches into an extended discussion that includes marital sex, celibacy, and divorce. Here Paul wishes that everyone could live as he does—namely, in celibacy (1 Cor 7:7). For this view Paul offers two reasons. The second isn't particularly surprising: marriage will distract believers from following Jesus (1 Cor 7:32-35). But Paul first justifies celibacy by reminding believers that "the time has drawn short" (7:29-31). If you're eager to enjoy sex, Paul advises, just hang on a little bit. Jesus will return soon!

> **Soon Enough?**
>
> Paul is famous for many things, among them his encouragement that, if possible, believers are better off pursuing celibacy rather than marriage (1 Cor 7). Paul provides two arguments for this advice, and one of them involves apocalyptic exhortation. The second argument involves the practical suggestion that marriage adds many concerns (or "anxieties") to life. Paul says these distractions draw men toward "the world's concerns" rather than "the Lord's concerns." Simply, a married man—Paul is speaking only to men here—will have less time for "things of the Lord" than will an unmarried man (1 Cor 7:32-34).
>
> But Paul's first argument is that "the time has drawn short" (1 Cor 7:29), with "the present crisis" on the horizon (7:26). He seems to be drawing upon the notion that a period of crisis would precede Jesus's return. Maybe it's easier to remain celibate if one expects the *parousia* to happen soon.

Why does Paul make so much of the cross and resurrection, a combination he mentions in other letters (especially Romans) but not in the strategic way he does in 1 Corinthians? I have suggested that Paul is seeking to undermine those believers who claim status based upon their spiritual attainments, and that the crucifixion demonstrates that God's saving work has nothing to do with status. Paul's appeal to the resurrection and return of Jesus complements that first argument. The Corinthians, or some of them, apparently believe they possess all the spiritual gifts they need; in reply, Paul insists that they have not yet arrived—nor will they until Jesus's return. This line of argument climaxes in 1 Corinthians 13. Paul famously argues that spiritual gifts like speaking in tongues and prophecy, gifts he discusses in chapters 12 and 14, pale in comparison to the gift of love. Love, Paul asserts, is permanent (13:8, 13). But at the return of Jesus tongues, knowledge, and prophecy all come to an end. "Now I know partially, but then I will know completely in he same way that I have been completely known" (1 Cor 13:12). Paul's expectation of a future resurrection and of Jesus's return means that no one has yet attained full status in the things of God. "If we have a hope in Christ only in this life, then we deserve to be pitied more than anyone else" (1 Cor 15:19).

> **Resurrection versus Resuscitation**
>
> In this section we discuss the resurrection of Jesus as exceptional: the biblical tradition includes no other examples of individual resurrection.
>
> Some readers may object: What about Lazarus? What about the widow's son raised by Elijah? And what about the others Jesus restores to life from apparent death? Those stories involve not resurrection but resuscitation. These stories feature persons who are restored to life but who will assuredly die again at some later point. Resurrection marks a permanent transformation: those who are raised will never die again.

Paul scatters references to Jesus's resurrection, return, and consummation of all things throughout his letters, but we gain valuable perspective from one particular section, Romans 6–8.[14] It's all but impossible to pull one thread from Paul's argument here without distorting the whole. This treatment is necessarily selective. Nevertheless, Romans 6–8 roams from the plight of individuals to the redemption of all creation—all through apocalyptic categories.

The section begins with a question: "Should we continue sinning so grace will multiply?" (Rom 6:1). Paul doesn't really mean it. He anticipates an objection to his message, namely that his emphasis on divine grace offers no motivation for ethical behavior. If God forgives freely, one might object, why pursue righteousness? Paul will argue that his gospel actually empowers ethical living.

Modern readers easily miss one essential point: Paul's argument depends upon a mystical and apocalyptic reality. In a mystical sense persons who reside in Christ participate—somehow[15]—in Christ's death and in the power of his resurrection.

> Therefore, we were buried together with [Christ] through baptism into his death, so that just as Christ was raised from the dead through the glory of the Father, we too can walk in newness of life. If we were united together in a death like his, we will also be united together in a resurrection like his. (Rom 6:4-5)

At the risk of restating the obvious, the very idea of resurrection crystallized in apocalyptic literature. And while Paul clearly has in view the experience of individuals, he writes in the first person plural: "We." In other words, the death and resurrection of Jesus bear upon a collective. Moreover, Paul moves from past to future language. (Greek did not have a "past" tense in the way that English does.)

The plural and past-future dimensions of Paul's language are significant. In Paul's day Jewish apocalyptic literature always spoke of resurrection as a corporate event that marked the end of the present age and the entry of the next. We find no references to the resurrection of individuals, only of all people or all righteous people all at once. So Jesus presents both an exception and a problem: a solitary individual who had been raised from the dead in the middle of the course of history. Early Christians, Paul included, had to figure out how to account for this. Paul's solution represents one common view. Jesus's resurrection marks the beginning of the end. Paul refers to it as the "first crop" (1 Cor 15:20, 23), as Jesus's resurrection actually begins the process of a general and final resurrection.

In other words, Jesus's past resurrection affects the present experience of believers. They actually participate in it to some degree. How that works exactly is difficult to explain.[16] Believers live differently because they already participate in Jesus's new life through the Holy Spirit. Just as Paul refers to Jesus as the first crop from the dead, he identifies the Spirit as the "first crop" of believers' hope (Rom 8:23), associating the Spirit's work with Jesus's resurrection (see Rom 8:11). Jesus's resurrection also promises future benefits, as it marks simply the beginning of a process that must see its consummation. So believers await their full resurrection (Rom 6:5).

If Jesus's resurrection marks a turning point in the experience of believers, it also implies future redemption for the entire cosmos. In chapter 8 Paul transitions from present suffering to future glory, from a focus on mortals to an emphasis that includes the entire creation (Rom 8:18-19), and back again from reflection on the entire creation to the ultimate fate of believers (8:31-39). Paul unites the frustration of a creation that must reckon with disorder with that of mortals who experience disorder in their own lives (Rom 8:22-23). Drawing upon an image fairly common in apocalyptic literature, Paul compares creation's frustration to a woman in the throes of delivering a baby (Rom 8:22). Mortals and creation alike await the "revealing" of God's children (Rom 8:19). Jesus's resurrection implies the consummation of all things.

In addition to the resurrection, *parousia*, consummation pattern, Paul also employs the language of *revelation* (Greek: *apokalypsis*). This usage is distinct from revelation in terms of a personal mystical experience. Rather, it has to do with "revealing" God's truth to the rest of the world. Paul mentions "the day of wrath" when "God's just judgment will be revealed" (Rom 2:5), the "revelation of God's sons and daughters" (8:19), and the revelation embodied by the gospel of Jesus (16:25; see 1 Cor 1:7)—language he employs only in Romans and (once) in 1 Corinthians.

Contrary to the popular impression of Paul, he spends little time talking about an apocalyptic topic like *judgment*—and he never mentions hell or eternal punishment. We should be careful with such a claim: we have already suggested that Paul's core message involves deliverance from the "coming wrath" (1 Thess 1:9-10; see Rom 5:9). Moreover, Paul absolutely believes in a final "day" when God will execute judgment (Rom 2:5; 2 Cor 5:10). Yet commonly Paul's references to wrath or judgment also refer to the natural consequences that ensnare a sinful humanity—and already do so on this side of death.[17] In Paul's classic statement on the topic, Romans 1:18-32, God's wrath has already been "revealed" in that God "abandoned" (1:24, 26, 28) misguided people to their own devices. In particular, sinful mortals find themselves enslaved to the powers of sin and death (see especially Rom 5:12-21). In Paul's understanding one reaps what one sows, with consequences for this life and the life beyond (Gal 6:7-9). His letters show no explicit interest in an eternal punishment for the wicked.

Apocalyptic Ends

Perhaps the most remarkable thing about Paul's apocalyptic language involves the variety of things he accomplishes with it.[18] Paul wrote letters in order to accomplish certain ends. Paul's letters reflect what Aristotle would have called *rhetoric*, "the faculty of observing in any given case the available means of persuasion."[19] Formally or informally, any man who enjoyed Paul's level of literacy would have encountered the common rhetorical conventions of the day, and Paul's letters demonstrate his rhetorical skill. Moreover, Paul's letters address diverse aims, often multiple aims within the same letter. For example, in Romans Paul is building a relationship with churches he has never visited, hoping to use them as a base of support for work to the west (Rom 15:23-28). But he also addresses conflict among Jewish and Gentile believers. Second Corinthians includes a section devoted to charitable fundraising (chaps. 8–9), a collection he mentions elsewhere (Rom 15:25-28; 1 Cor 16:1-4; Gal 2:10), but he begins by defending himself against charges that his conduct lacks integrity (1:12). Philippians fosters unity within the church—and it offers thanks for gifts Paul has received. In short, the occasional nature of Paul's letters implies that we should pay attention to their rhetorical nature. Here we will sketch several functions to which Paul applies apocalyptic discourse—providing a single example for each.

1. We've already observed Paul appealing to apocalyptic categories to *correct* his audience in 1 Corinthians. We only hear Paul's side of the conversation, so we can only guess as to the actual circumstances or the perceptions of those who received the letter. In any case Paul addresses a group marked by sharp divisions (1 Cor 1:10-12) that have to do with status: some believers regard themselves as more gifted than others (see especially chaps. 12–14). Paul replies by emphasizing apocalyptic eschatology. Some among the Corinthians may be wise, but the crucifixion reveals that people of this age cannot discern true wisdom from folly (1 Cor 2:7-8). (This perspective only makes sense in the light of Jesus's resurrection and return.) The Corinthians have indeed received gifts, but none of them has attained the full measure of blessing that will come with Jesus's return (1 Cor 13:8-12). Whatever maturity the Corinthians may have attained, the final resurrection still awaits them (15:1-58).

2. We have also noted how Paul relies upon his own apocalyptic revelations to buttress his *authority* against opposition from competing Christian teachers. In 2 Corinthians 12:1-10 Paul relates his journey to the third heaven, among other "visions and revelations from the Lord." He implies that his "foolish" boasting underscores his superiority over against competing "super-apostles" who teach a "different gospel" (2 Cor 11:4-5). In Galatians Paul again confronts what he regards as "another gospel" (1:6-9). There he appeals to a different set of revelatory experiences. His first encounter with the risen Jesus provided divine authorization for Paul's message (1:12, 15-16). And when he faced possible conflict with the more established church leaders in Jerusalem, he visited them not because he *needed* to but "because of a revelation" (2:2).

3. One obvious use for apocalyptic discourse involves *comfort*, as apocalyptic eschatology promises a future better than the highly problematic present. The classic example occurs in 1 Thessalonians 4:13-18. Modern readers may find this passage confusing, especially depending upon the translation they use. Paul begins by saying he wants to inform the Thessalonians concerning those who have died. (Many translations read, "those who have fallen

asleep.") He goes on to explain that upon Jesus's return those who have died, along with believers who remain alive, will meet Jesus in the air—"that way we will always be with the Lord." "So," he concludes, "encourage each other with these words." Most interpreters understand Paul as speaking to a concern that has emerged among the Thessalonians: if a believer dies before Jesus's return, will they miss out on eternal salvation? (Could it be that Paul has not addressed this issue already?) We may readily imagine the anxiety that attends such a question. What about loved ones who have died? And what about *me*, should I die before Jesus's return? Paul seeks to comfort the Thessalonians by insisting that those who have died enter the same future as those who remain living upon Jesus's return.

4. Paul continues with apocalyptic topics in 1 Thessalonians, moving on to *exhort* or *encourage* them to maintain their enthusiasm as they await the *parousia* (1 Thess 5:1-11). This too is a fairly obvious and common usage for apocalyptic discourse. "The day of the Lord is going to come like a thief in the night," Paul warns (1 Thess 5:2). He may have gotten this line from traditions going back to Jesus. (See Matt 24:42-44.) Paul goes on with a pep talk: the Thessalonians don't want to be surprised by Jesus's return. Instead, they should remain watchful.

5. If eagerness for Jesus's return might inspire faithful living, the prospect of divine judgment can frighten or *admonish* people to behave in particular ways. In Romans 14 Paul faces a conflict in the church regarding what believers may or may not eat, along with some other divisive issues. Paul acknowledges the disagreements, but he wants the Roman believers to rise above them and live out a greater unity. "Why do you judge your brother or sister?" he asks. "We all will stand in front of the judgment seat of God," and "each of us will give an account of ourselves to God" (Rom 14:10-12). Divisive, judgmental behavior opens persons to the judgment that comes from God, Paul reasons. One wants to avoid that (see 1 Cor 4:1-5).

The Whole Enchilada

Often people associate apocalyptic discourse with individualistic religious hope. Passed down to us through Western culture, this association identifies apocalyptic thought with the question of what happens to people after they die. Do they go to heaven, or do they go to hell? With judgment meted out on such an individualized basis, the apocalyptic message boils down to one of two messages. Warning: you'd better get your act together if you want to avoid hell. And comfort: It's okay; things eventually get better.

Paul surely discusses judgment—sometimes wrath—and the afterlife. He does take great comfort in afterlife hope. Living is Christ, after all, but dying is gain (Phil 1:21). Yet Paul never pauses to reflect on the nature of hell. (Many readers will find this surprising.) He hardly has anything to say about heaven. When he does get specific about life beyond death, he talks in terms of transformation (1 Cor 15:51-52) and being in the presence of—"knowing" and being "known" by—Christ (1 Thess 4:17; 1 Cor 13:12; Phil 3:10). Without question Paul is interested in individual salvation. "If we have hope in Christ only in this life, then we deserve to be pitied more than anyone else" (1 Cor 15:19).

Often overlooked, however, is the breadth of Paul's apocalyptic vision. In Romans 8 Paul laments the bondage, pain, and frustration to which the entire cosmos has been subjected. God will surely, Paul says, set the creation free (Rom 8:21). Here Paul uses language that implies a connection between Jesus's resurrection and the renewal of creation: he calls believers' experience of the Holy Spirit the "first crop" of a greater redemption (Rom 8:23). Paul links the Holy Spirit with life and resurrection (see Rom 1:4; 8:10-11). This language is significant because Paul elsewhere identifies Jesus's resurrection as the "first crop" of a greater resurrection (1 Cor 15:23). Paul immediately moves from Jesus's resurrection, the "first crop," to the subjection of all things under Christ (1 Cor 15:20-28). For Paul, Jesus's resurrection marks the beginning of life and renewal for the entire cosmos.

Paul's broad vision might even extend to what we would call universalism, the expectation that all people will receive salvation. This is a controversial topic in Pauline studies. Not many interpreters believe Paul was a thoroughgoing universalist. It is difficult to see Paul as a universalist, for example, when he refers to the "day of wrath" (Rom 2:5-10; see Rom 9:22; 1 Thess 1:10), discusses people who are being destroyed (1 Cor 1:18; 2 Cor 2:15; 4:3), and identifies those who cannot enter the kingdom of God (1 Cor 6:9-10; Gal 5:21).

The textual evidence for a universalist Paul is very slim, but it relies heavily upon Paul's apocalyptic reasoning, a logical flow that is quite compelling. On two occasions Paul refers to Christ as the second Adam: just as Adam's sin brought death to all people, Paul reasons, so Christ's resurrection brings life to everyone. Paul says this most clearly in 1 Corinthians 15:22: "in the same way that everyone dies in Adam, so also everyone will be given life in Christ." Paul seems less certain when he draws the same analogy in Romans. Here I'll attempt a literal translation (with italics for emphasis) of a complicated argument.

> But death reigned from Adam until Moses, even upon those who had not sinned in the fashion of the transgression of Adam, who is a *type* of the one to come. But the gift is unlike the transgression. For if *many* died through the transgression of one [man], much more did the grace and the gift of God abound for *many* in the one man Jesus Christ. And the gift is not like the effect of the one man's sin. For the judgment from the one [brings] condemnation, but the gift from many trespasses [brings] justification. For if in the transgression of one [man] death reigned through that one, much more will *those who receive* the abundance of grace and the gift of righteousness rule through the one, Jesus Christ. Therefore just as through the transgression of one [comes] judgment for *all*, even so through the righteousness of one [comes] justification that leads to life for *all* people. (Rom 5:14-18)

The translation above includes several close judgments on my part, but it calls particular attention to the nature of the relationship Paul establishes between Adam and Jesus—and it sets forth the key reasons interpreters debate this passage. First, Paul names Adam a "type" of Jesus. That is, in some significant way Paul finds a meaningful relationship or correspondence between Adam and Jesus. Second, and more problematically, Paul moves from the language of *many* to the language of *all* within the passage. Does the typological relationship between Adam and Jesus apply to *everyone* or simply to *many*? Paul cannot regard Adam as greater than

Jesus. Logically, then, how could one argue that Adam's sin creates death for *everyone* while Jesus's righteousness brings life only for *many*? Finally, we observe that Paul refers to "those who receive" Christ's benefits—as if some do receive those benefits but others do not.

The typological reasoning Paul establishes between Adam and Jesus suggests that Paul was a universalist. Adam's transgression may have brought death to humankind, but Christ's righteousness and resurrection are even more powerful. So it seems in 1 Corinthians 15:22 and perhaps—but only perhaps—in Romans 5:14-22. However we see things with respect to the salvation of individuals, Paul's apocalyptic gospel encompasses a much broader scope. Through Jesus and his resurrection, God is inaugurating the renewal of all things.

Beyond This Age, Beyond Death: Paul's Developing Thought

In 1 Thessalonians and 1 Corinthians Paul clearly expects to be alive when Jesus returns. "All of us won't die," he writes, "but we will all be changed" (1 Cor 15:51; see 1 Thess 4:17). Paul, of course, is keenly conscious of his own mortality. After all, he reports painful, sometimes deadly persecution at several points in his life. He discusses "being handed over to death for Jesus' sake" (2 Cor 4:11) and the like on multiple occasions. But 1 Corinthians and 1 Thessalonians may represent the two earliest Pauline epistles available to us—and they both convey the impression that Paul expects still to be living at the *parousia*.

We get a different impression when we turn to Philippians. Not only did Paul likely write Philippians later in his career, Philippians is one of his "prison epistles." Paul discusses his imprisonment (Phil 1:7, 17), going so far as to claim that his confinement has actually helped to spread the gospel (1:12-14). But ancient imprisonment scarcely resembled incarceration in a modern democratic society. One did not receive a formal sentence for a crime. Instead, ancient authorities used prisons to contain a prisoner's body until it was deemed appropriate to release that person: perhaps after the prisoner no longer represented a threat to public order, perhaps after the prisoner had received "enough" punishment, including torture.

English translations obscure that Paul refers to his imprisonment as his "chains," suggesting both an abysmal prison setting and possibly (this is often overlooked) significant physical pain. Let's just say ancient prisons lacked modern public health accommodations. As a prisoner Paul has no idea when he may be released, and he wonders whether he will survive. He depends on his friends, including the Philippians, to look after many of his needs (Phil 2:25-30; 4:10-20).

This background may explain why Philippians reflects different expectations regarding Paul's fate than do 1 Thessalonians and 1 Corinthians. If he dies as a prisoner or suffers execution, Paul wants to be "like" Christ in his death "so that I may perhaps reach the goal of the resurrection of the dead" (Phil 3:10-11).

Paul still awaits the resurrection, only now he anticipates that he may die before Jesus's return. But another passage in Philippians suggests that Paul may have changed his mind to an even greater degree. I quote the passage in full, providing my own translation.

> For I know that this will lead to salvation for me through your prayers and the help of the Spirit of Jesus Christ, according to my eager expectation and hope, that in no way will I be put to shame but with boldness, as always and even now, Christ will be exalted in my body whether through my life or through my death. For to me, to live is Christ and to die is gain. If I am to live in the flesh, this is fruitful work for me, and I do not know which I prefer. I am hard pressed between the two, having the desire to depart and be with Christ, which is far better, but to remain in the flesh is more necessary for you. (Phil 1:19-24)

Here Paul seems to express his hope differently. Rather than awaiting a resurrection that occurs upon Jesus's return, the expectation we find in 1 Corinthians and 1 Thessalonians, he apparently anticipates that death takes one directly into Christ's presence.

Early Jews and Christians expressed diverse views concerning the afterlife.[20] Within the New Testament Luke apparently assumes that people reach their final fate immediately upon death (Luke 16:19-31; 23:43; perhaps Acts 7:59), but Matthew teaches a final resurrection and sorting at the end of the age (Matt 13:36-43, 49-50; 25:31-46). Only in Matthew "the bodies of many holy people" are raised at the moment of Jesus's death and wander through Jerusalem, suggesting that the righteous dead remain just that—dead—until the final hour (27:52-53). The Book of Revelation seems to blend both views: martyrs go directly into Christ's presence (Rev 6:9-11), while most of the dead must await the final judgment (20:11-15). Perhaps this is what Paul has in mind: that as a martyr he would depart immediately into Christ's presence, but otherwise the righteous dead "sleep" until Jesus's return.

Could it be that Paul has changed his mind from a belief in a final resurrection to hope that people reach their ultimate fate upon their death? Or does Paul share the view we find in Revelation, that martyrs receive special treatment?

Beyond Paul

Paul's interpreters routinely face a major decision: of the thirteen New Testament epistles that bear Paul's name, how many did he actually write? This question may seem obscure, but our answers will shape how we understand Paul on many important questions. For example, did Paul believe in salvation apart from good works? Did Paul exhort wives to submit to their husbands and slaves to obey their masters? Did Paul establish formal offices in the churches he founded, including procedures and criteria for identifying appropriate candidates? Not many scholars believe Paul actually wrote the Pastoral Epistles: 1 Timothy, 2 Timothy, and Titus. (Second Timothy is a more complicated case than many people realize.) Most interpreters are suspicious regarding Paul's authorship of Ephesians, Colossians, and 2 Thessalonians—but here opinion is more evenly divided. Our judgments of these questions bear implications for understanding how Paul related to apocalyptic eschatology as well.

Pseudonymity

The term *pseudonymity* applies to instances in which one person (or group) writes under the name of another. Sometimes pseudonymity is simply a writing convention, as occurs in modern satire and perhaps in the act of attributing wisdom writings to King Solomon. All the ancient Jewish apocalypses are pseudonymous. And

> sometimes pseudonymity runs closer to forgery: intentional efforts to deceive an audience, often for political or financial gain.
>
> Pseudonymity was common in the ancient world, no less so in Judaism and Christianity. We have already mentioned several texts written in Paul's name in the second century and beyond. Readers must develop their own moral assessments of these practices.[21]

In my opinion Paul probably wrote none of the six "disputed" epistles. I suggest we look at these things from another angle: What if we considered Ephesians, Colossians, 2 Thessalonians, 1 Timothy, 2 Timothy, and Titus as *interpretations* and *adaptations* of Paul? Later believers took their best understandings of Paul and asked, "What would Paul say if he were here?" Perhaps some exercised more freedom in answering those questions than others, but it helps us understand all six of these letters as early interpretations of Paul's own eschatological teaching on two important matters.

First, there's the matter of "realized" versus "inaugurated" eschatology. People who hold a realized eschatology believe that Jesus's resurrection has already brought all its benefits to believers. Believers are already "saved"; they have already transcended sin's hold on their lives. (As an extreme example, some popular televangelists promote the idea that faithful believers should never suffer disease.) The opposite of a realized eschatology would be a "future" eschatology, in which believers receive the benefits of salvation only after Jesus's return. An inaugurated eschatology understands the present moment as mixed: Jesus's resurrection already gives life and power to believers—its blessings have already been *inaugurated*—yet believers still await their final redemption from sin, oppression, and death.

In his undisputed letters Paul promotes an inaugurated eschatology, insisting that believers live in anticipation of Jesus's return. He argues this matter most forcefully in Romans and (especially) 1 Corinthians, but it emerges in other letters as well. In Philippians, for example, Paul expresses hope that "I may perhaps reach the goal of the resurrection of the dead." Right away, however, he reminds the Philippians that he has not yet attained this: "It's not that I have already reached this goal or have already been perfected, but I pursue it, so that I may grab hold of it…" (3:11-12).

One wonders: does Paul anticipate that people will likely mistake his confidence for a realized eschatology?

Earlier in this chapter we considered Paul's arguments concerning the resurrection in 1 Corinthians. He begins the letter by acknowledging that "in everything" the Corinthians have been blessed, in both speech and knowledge; moreover, they are not "missing any spiritual gift." Yet Paul slyly qualifies this praise by adding, "while you wait for our Lord Jesus Christ to be revealed" (1 Cor 1:5-7). Indeed, the entire letter seems to argue that spiritual gifts are great—but they do not represent the fullness of salvation. The Corinthians may have received knowledge and other spiritual gifts, but love is even greater (1 Cor 8:1; 13:1-3); moreover, those gifts remain incomplete until Jesus returns (13:8-12). By no coincidence Paul closes the letter with his longest reflection on the significance of Jesus's return and a final resurrection (15:1-58).

> **Pseudonymity in Ephesians and Colossians?**
>
> The position that Paul did not write Ephesians or Colossians is held by a slim to a substantial majority of interpreters. In the eyes of most interpreters, however, the question of authorship seems much more challenging for these two letters than it does for the Pastoral Epistles. Eschatology plays a major role in those discussions.
>
> An especially helpful discussion of these questions may be found in the chapters on Ephesians and Colossians in Raymond Brown's textbook *An Introduction to the New Testament* (New York: Doubleday, 1997).

Paul builds similar arguments in Romans. There he acknowledges the plight of humanity and of the world. Despite the resurrection, humans still live in a broken world and suffer along with it. They await final redemption for all things (Rom 8:18-30).

Yet two of the disputed epistles, Colossians and especially Ephesians, may encourage a different impression. Readers will decide for themselves how much Ephesians builds upon Paul's language from Romans: in baptism believers have joined Christ in death to sin, making it possible for them to "walk in newness of life" (Rom 6:4). Again Paul adds a qualification with a classic statement of inaugurated eschatology: believers *have been* united with Jesus in death, but they *will be* united in his resurrection (Rom 6:5). Ephesians presses Paul beyond that boundary toward a more realized eschatology: God has already "brought us to life with Christ," having already raised believers up and seated them with Christ in the heavenly places (Eph 2:5-6). But then Ephesians pulls back a bit: in "future generations," Ephesians argues, God will reveal great blessings (2:7). Some interpreters see Ephesians moving beyond Paul's inaugurated eschatology to more of a realized eschatology; perhaps the distinction is subtle, but at this point it seems that the perspective of Ephesians runs closer to the position Paul criticized in 1 Corinthians than it does to Paul's own understanding. Other interpreters find Ephesians more compatible with Romans.

For its part, Colossians never refers to Jesus's return. While Paul identifies the believers' resurrection with Jesus as a future event (Rom 6:4-5), Colossians and Ephesians identify the resurrection of believers as having been already accomplished (Col 2:12; 3:1)—but again Colossians looks forward to a future revelation (3:4): "When Christ, who is your life, is revealed, then you also will be revealed with him in glory." Like Ephesians, Colossians at first seems to modify Paul's theology by celebrating the blessings believers have already received, then returns to place hope in the future.

Ephesians and Colossians represent complex cases, but we encounter a more clear line of development from the undisputed Paul in 2 Thessalonians and two of the Pastoral Epistles. Many ancient apocalyptic texts describe a period of great distress that occurs just prior to the age of salvation. This scenario commonly identifies the present age or the near future as a time of tribulation or apostasy. For example, Jesus's apocalyptic speeches in the Synoptic Gospels warn of such an ordeal (see Matt 24; Mark 13; Luke 21). Paul's undisputed letters, however, do not. Paul does lament the "present evil age" (Gal 1:4) and "the present suffering" (Rom 8:18; see 2 Cor 4:17). But the undisputed letters do not provide a script in which a particular period of distress precedes God's final intervention in history. They certainly do not present a scenario according to which people may reckon or calculate the time of Jesus's return. That event, Paul says, "is going to come like a thief in the night" (1 Thess 5:2).

Second Thessalonians and the Pastorals, however, do set forth scenarios in which a period of apostasy (or falling away from faith) marks the last days. Second Thessalonians picks up on a concern expressed in 1 Thessalonians 5:1-11, that complacency might set in as believers await Jesus's return, warning that a great apostasy must precede Jesus's coming, accompanied by a "son of destruction" who will receive worship in the Jerusalem temple (2 Thess 2:3; my translation). The tradition of an end-time villain who corrupts the temple goes back at least to the book of Daniel (9:27; 11:31; 12:11) and appears in Jesus's eschatological speeches (Matt 24:15; Mark 13:14; modified in Luke 21:20). In 2 Thessalonians this "lawless man" (my translation) is only temporarily restrained by Satan before he will face destruction at the coming of Jesus. It's quite the scenario (2 Thess 2:3-10), and it's complemented by additional detailed information: Jesus's return is accompanied by angels "with blazing fire" and destruction against those who do not obey the gospel (2 Thess 1:7-10). This language, too, does not occur in the undisputed letters.

First and Second Timothy don't follow the same script we find in 2 Thessalonians, but both letters do discuss an end-time apostasy. "In later times" some people will fall away from the faith by attending to false teachings, warns 1 Timothy (4:1-3). And in "the last days" difficult times will come, including the deception of "immature women," according to 2 Timothy (3:1-9). In coming days people will prefer user-friendly instruction over against the truth (2 Tim 4:3-4). Again, Paul's undisputed letters never go into that level of detail when discussing the end times.

In short, in the eyes of many interpreters Ephesians, Colossians, 2 Thessalonians, and the Pastoral Epistles modify Paul's apocalyptic eschatology. The undisputed Paul promoted an *inaugurated* eschatology that withheld the fullness of Christ's blessings until the *parousia*. By contrast, some say, Ephesians and Colossians advance a more *realized* eschatology, in which believers have already been raised to live with Christ. Second Thessalonians and the Pastorals provide a more detailed end-time scenario than does the undisputed Paul, particularly with a period of apostasy marking the last days.

Conclusion

The Apostle Paul represents our earliest literary witness to the Christian movement. Although Paul never wrote a theological textbook, or even a systematic presentation of his beliefs, a strong apocalyptic core animated his message. Paul not only preached Jesus's death, he also announced Jesus's resurrection, return, and ultimate triumph over death and evil. Paul adapted this core message to a variety of contexts and problems, using apocalyptic discourse to correct his opponents, support his own authority, comfort anxious believers, exhort communities to faithful discipleship, and admonish wayward members of his churches. In contrast to the popular view that Paul preached a gospel of individual salvation, his apocalyptic vision included the renewal of the cosmos and (perhaps) the salvation of all people.

But Paul's apocalyptic message may not have held static. As he got older he encountered the likelihood that he might die before Jesus's return. In response to this reality perhaps Paul adapted his understanding of what happens when we die from a belief that the dead simply remain dead until Jesus's return to a hope that upon death he might immediately be taken into the presence of Jesus. Moreover, some of Paul's later admirers—whose writings we find in the disputed epistles—may have adapted his theology by moving toward a more realized eschatology (Ephesians and Colossians) and by adding a detailed scenario of apostasy and crisis prior to Jesus's return (2 Thessalonians and the Pastorals).

For Further Reading

Allison, Dale C. *Jesus of Nazareth: Millenarian Prophet.* Minneapolis: Fortress Press, 1998.

Bassler, Jouette M. *Navigating Paul: An Introduction to Key Theological Concepts.* Louisville: Westminster John Knox, 2007.

Beker, J. Christiaan. *Paul the Apostle: The Triumph of God in Life and Thought.* Philadelphia: Fortress Press, 1980.

Boyarin, Daniel. *A Radical Jew: Paul and the Politics of Identity.* Berkeley: University of California Press, 1994.

Brown, Alexandra R. *The Cross and Human Transformation: Paul's Apocalyptic Word in 1 Corinthians.* Minneapolis: Fortress Press, 1995.

Campbell, Douglas M. *The Deliverance of God: An Apocalyptic Rereading of Justification in Paul.* Grand Rapids: Eerdmans, 2009.

Carey, Greg. *Elusive Apocalypse: Reading Authority in the Revelation to John.* StABH 15. Macon, GA: Mercer University Press, 1999.

Charlesworth, James H. "Paradise." Pages 4.377–78 in *NIDB.* Nashville: Abingdon Press, 2009.

de Boer, M. C. "Paul and Apocalyptic Eschatology." Pages 345–83 in *The Encyclopedia of Apocalypticism, Volume 1: The Origins of Apocalypticism in Judaism and Christianity.* Ed. John J. Collins. New York: Continuum, 1998.

Dunn, James D. G. *The Theology of Paul the Apostle.* Grand Rapids: Eerdmans, 1998.

Ehrman, Bart D. *Forged: Writing in the Name of God—Why the Bible's Authors Are Not Who We Think They Are.* New York: HarperCollins, 2011.

Gaventa, Beverly Roberts, ed. *Apocalyptic Paul: Cosmos and Anthropos in Romans 5–8.* Waco, TX: Baylor University Press, 2013.

Martyn, J. Louis. *Theological Issues in the Letters of Paul.* Nashville: Abingdon Press, 1997.

Meeks, Wayne A. "Social Functions of Apocalyptic Language in Pauline Christianity." Pages 687–705 in *Apocalypticism in the Mediterranean World and the Near East: Proceedings from the International Colloquium on Apocalypticism, Uppsala, August 12-17, 1979.* Tübingen: Mohr (Siebeck), 1983.

Roetzel, Calvin. *Paul: The Man and the Myth.* Studies on Personalities of the New Testament. Minneapolis: Fortress Press, 1999.

Taylor, Walter F., Jr. *Paul: Apostle to the Nations: An Introduction.* Minneapolis: Fortress Press, 2012.

Wright, N. T. *The New Testament and the People of God.* Minneapolis: Fortress Press, 1992.

Chapter Four
The Synoptic Take(s) on Jesus

Mark's Gospel jumps immediately—well, almost immediately—into Jesus's career. There's no genealogy, no infancy narrative. Instead we readers enter a strange scene: out in the wilderness John the Baptist is baptizing people in the Jordan River "for the forgiveness of sins" (Mark 1:4 NRSV). John's appearance enhances the strangeness of the moment, wearing a camel's-hair garment and a leather belt, and his locust-and-wild-honey diet grabs the attention as well. The leather belt in particular reminds readers of Elijah, the greatest of Israel's prophets (2 Kings 1:8). Then comes Jesus to receive John's baptism.

A Hollywood production might begin differently. Following the lead of Matthew or Luke, it might open with Jesus's birth, or perhaps Mary's pregnancy: remarkable signs portending a singular life. Alternatively, it might lead with one of Jesus's great deeds: a healing story, perhaps, filmed through the eyes of a crippled man or woman. Wouldn't it be interesting to start with a controversy, with critics accusing Jesus of violating the law by healing on the Sabbath? Mark, however, introduces Jesus out in the wilderness for his encounter with John at the Jordan.

Nearly all scholars agree that Mark's Gospel sets the agenda for Matthew and Luke. We identify Matthew, Mark, and Luke as the *Synoptic Gospels* because they so often "see" (syn-optic = see together) Jesus's story in common ways—and because we too, by "seeing" these three Gospels side by side, can observe their remarkable similarities and divergences. The still-dominant view has it that Mark is the earliest of the surviving gospels and that Matthew and Luke individually used Mark as the basis for their own stories. This model recognizes that Matthew and Luke also share a significant block of material that is absent from Mark. Interpreters typically attribute that material to a now-lost, and therefore hypothetical, source we call *Q*—an abbreviation for the German *Quelle*, which simply means "source." We call this model for explaining the relationships among Matthew, Mark, and Luke the *Two-Source Hypothesis*: Mark and Q came first, then Matthew and Luke built their stories around Mark's framework while inserting Q material at various locations.

In this book we assume *Marcan Priority*, the belief that Mark provides a framework for Matthew and Luke. Very few scholars reject the idea that Mark provides the framework for Matthew and Luke. A growing minority, however, rejects the idea of a Q source. According to this group, Mark influenced Matthew and then Luke worked from Matthew (or from Matthew and Mark) rather than from Q. The apparent precedence of Mark is why we begin with the apocalyptic dimensions of Mark's story. Then we'll move on to examine how Matthew and Luke take Mark's apocalyptic framework and create their own spin. We will address Q in more detail in the next chapter.

Mark's Apocalyptic Storyline

Apocalyptic expectation pervades Mark's wild scene with Jesus meeting John in the wilderness. The wilderness setting provides the first element. Mark combines quotes from Malachi 3:1 and Isaiah 40:3, passages that involve the return of Judah's exiles from Babylon. Both passages envision a glorious new day in Jerusalem. Apparently apocalyptically minded Jews picked up especially on Isaiah 40:3, interpreting it as preparation for God's ultimate deliverance of Israel. The Dead Sea Scrolls' *Community Rule* (1QS 8:13-15) draws upon Isaiah 40:3 in explaining why the community at Qumran has abandoned Jerusalem to study the law in the desert in preparation for a final judgment. John gathers people in the desert and baptizes them in repentance and as preparation for the "one who is coming" (1:7, literal translation). As M. Eugene Boring puts it,

> This repentance is not an individualistic being-sorry for one's personal wrongdoings—though it does not exclude that—but a joining in the corporate renewal of the people of God preparing for God's eschatological act.[1]

For this symbolic moment John chooses not just any body of water but the Jordan River. The Jordan evokes memories of God's defining act of salvation in the past, Israel's deliverance from slavery in Egypt. When, after forty years of wandering, the people cross over to take possession of their new land, it's the Jordan they must cross. Eugene Boring again:

> As Israel had once come out of the wilderness, passed through the waters of the Jordan, and settled in Judea and Jerusalem, now the whole people are pictured as returning to the wilderness, passing through the waters of the Jordan, confessing their former sinfulness, and reemerging as the nucleus of the renewed people of God.[2]

The whole setup creates a sense of eschatological anticipation: what is God about to do? Jesus arrives as the "coming one," and drama breaks out at the moment of his baptism. Mark's Greek tells us that when Jesus comes up out of the water "immediately" he sees the heavens ripped apart and the Spirit descending upon him like a dove. A heavenly voice speaks: "You are my Son, whom I dearly love; in you I find happiness" (Mark 1:11).

The scene raises difficult questions. First, Jesus sees the heavens tear and the Spirit descending, but are we to understand this as his private experience? And does anyone else hear the heavenly voice? We might compare the apocalyptic experience of Daniel, who experiences a vision in the company of others who do not perceive it (Dan 10:7).

Other apocalyptic overtones come through more clearly. Many readers will overlook one detail. Jesus has an apocalyptic vision: the heavens *rip apart* (Mark 1:10). Seeing into the heavenly realms constitutes a standard apocalyptic motif. For example, in Revelation 4:1 John sees a door open in the heavens, and he ascends to experience the remainder of his vision from that vantage point (see Ezek 1:1). Mark does even more with this image.

The Greek verb here, *schizō*, occurs just one other time in Mark. At the very moment of Jesus's death, the curtain of the temple rips apart (Mark 15:38). Then a centurion, who presumably has no idea about the curtain, proclaims, "This man was certainly God's Son" (15:39). In other words, there's tearing at the moment we first meet Jesus in Mark and at the moment of his death. Tearing frames Jesus's career. And it's not just ordinary tearing. A rip in the sky opens the boundary that separates God's dwelling place from the world. Likewise, a rip in the temple curtain opens a boundary between God's sacred space and the rest of the world. Not only does Jesus experience an apocalyptic vision, the motif of tearing frames Jesus's life with the proclamation that he is God's Son (Mark 1:10-11; 15:38-39).

The Spirit's descent might be better characterized as an eschatological detail rather than an apocalyptic one. John has already announced that the coming one would baptize people with the Holy Spirit. The Spirit is hardly a new concept in biblical traditions, but in some instances its arrival is associated with the last days. We see this same application in Acts 2:16-18, in which Peter announces the pouring out of the Spirit as a sign of the last days. (Here Acts quotes Joel 2:28-29, but the Greek text of Joel locates the Spirit's blessing "after these things," and the Hebrew "after this," rather than "in the last days.") Paul likewise describes the Spirit as the eschatological first fruits (Rom 8:23). At Jesus's baptism we encounter a motif that was relatively new in Judaism: the idea of a messiah upon whom the Spirit rests. Several texts from the period, all of which feature heavy doses of apocalyptic discourse—*Psalms of Solomon* 17:37; *Testament of Levi* 18:7-12; and *1 Enoch* 49:2-3—attest to this concept.[3]

At Jesus's baptism a heavenly voice announces him as God's Son, the Beloved One. Both concepts, Son of God and Beloved One, conveyed messianic overtones in first-century Judaism. As we have already seen, Jewish messianic speculation emerged most clearly within apocalyptic literature. Jesus's identification here as Son of God plays a critical role in the development of Mark's story. Mark probably began, "The beginning of the gospel of Jesus the messiah" (my translation), with the phrase "Son of God" lacking in important early manuscripts. But Jesus's identity as God's Son is extremely important for this Gospel. Until the moment of Jesus's death (Mark 15:39), only supernatural agents perceive this truth about Jesus. We hear it from the heavenly voice here, and again from demons on two occasions (Mark 3:11; 5:7). Just after Peter identifies Jesus as the messiah in 8:29, a heavenly voice again identifies Jesus as Son of God (9:7). Jesus indirectly refers to himself as Son on one occasion (Mark 13:32); at his trial he confesses himself as "Son of the blessed one" (14:61-62). We might say that Mark's Gospel is all about what Jesus's identity as messiah, Son of Man, and Son of God means. Heavenly voices and demons convey this message through apocalyptic imagery.

Mark intensifies the aura of eschatological expectation when "at once" the Spirit drives Jesus into the wilderness to face temptation by Satan (Mark 1:12). The wilderness setting—and the period of forty days—alludes to Israel's forty years in the wilderness as it journeyed from Egypt to the promised land. In this battle of supernatural forces Satan tests Jesus while angels serve him (Mark 1:12-13). Again, in Judaism interest in Satan and the angels, including their conflicts, first appears in apocalyptic discourse. Indeed, Jesus's very first miracle involves not the healing of an illness or disability but an exorcism (Mark 1:21-28). Conflict with supernatural forces will mark Jesus's ministry. Moreover, mystical experiences like the one Jesus has often happen outside: Ezekiel encounters God's fiery throne chariot beside a river (Ezek 1:1) and the dry bones in a valley (chap. 37), while Daniel receives an important vision beside the Tigris (Dan 10:4).

Finally, Jesus's initial message mirrors John's apocalyptic tenor. "Now is the time! Here comes God's kingdom! Change your hearts and lives, and trust this good news!" (Mark 1:15). Jesus, like John, is preparing Israel for God's imminent intervention in history.

Right from the start, then, Mark sets Jesus within the framework of Jewish apocalyptic discourse. John the Baptist preaches repentance in expectation of the coming one and the Holy Spirit. Through a personal revelation Jesus sees into the open heavens and hears a divine voice. The Holy Spirit's arrival marks him as the end-time messiah. An announcement that Jesus is God's Son and Beloved creates the expectation that the age of salvation is near. Jesus's wilderness temptation not only extends his mystical experience, it also places him in a conflict among supernatural forces. Jesus's own message continues the theme, calling people to prepare for God's coming kingdom.

These first scenes in Mark set the tone for the story that follows in several respects. For example, Jesus's vision of the opened heavens at his baptism stands as the first of two dramatic visionary experiences. Later Jesus tells a crowd, "I assure you that some standing here won't die before they see God's kingdom arrive in power" (Mark 9:1). He then takes three of his disciples alone, where they see him "transformed." Jesus's garments become radiantly white, and two great figures of Israel's past, Moses and Elijah, appear talking with Jesus. At this point the three disciples receive an additional revelation: a cloud overshadows them, and a heavenly voice calls out, "This is my Son, whom I dearly love. Listen to him!" (9:7). In both revelations, the one Jesus experiences at his baptism and the transfiguration, a divine voice reinforces the message that Jesus is God's Son. We won't hear that language again until Jesus's trial, when the high priest asks Jesus, "Are you the Christ, the Son of the blessed one?" and Jesus replies, "I am" (Mark 14:61-62). Apart from demons (see below), the only other voice to confirm Jesus's identity as Son of God is also linked to Jesus's baptism: the centurion pronounces Jesus Son of God just after the *tearing* of the temple curtain (15:38-39). Mark combines the visionary moments of Jesus's baptism and transfiguration, along with a couple of other passages, to reveal Jesus's identity as God's Son.

We might consider a second example of how Mark continues the apocalyptic overtones of its introduction. Jesus sends twelve of his disciples on a mission to do the very things he's been doing (Mark 6:7-13). He begins by giving them authority over unclean spirits, or demons. He sends them from village to village, and they preach that people should repent—an echo of John's message and the message with which Jesus himself begins (Mark 1:4, 15). Indeed, the twelve do exorcise "many" demons and heal many sick people. Jesus himself encounters opposition from supernatural forces: indeed, throughout most of the story only demons correctly recognize Jesus's identity (Mark 1:23-24, 34; 3:11; 5:7), and even Jesus's enemies take note of his power over demons (3:22).

Encounters with Satan and the demons constitute only one of several varieties of conflict Jesus experiences throughout Mark. He encounters resistance from various religious authorities and from the Roman governor Pilate, but he also clashes with some surprising groups. Over forty times Mark mentions the crowds, and Jesus is often trying to flee from them. Some of Mark's most memorable healing stories occur when Jesus is trying to avoid people (Mark 1:40-45; 2:1-12; 5:24-34; 7:24-30). Jesus's own disciples sometimes succeed, but as the Gospel progresses they repeatedly demonstrate their lack of faith and understanding. After the *second* miracle in which Jesus feeds a great crowd with meager resources, the disciples worry that they haven't brought enough bread. "You still don't understand?" Jesus wonders (Mark 8:21). And when Jesus attempts to prepare the disciples for his fate, but Peter tries to correct him, Jesus responds, "Get behind me, Satan" (8:33). By the story's end, all of his male disciples have fled in fear (14:50); even the women who follow Jesus to the cross flee at the message of his resurrection (16:8). Jesus also sparks conflict with his own family (3:21-31).

In Mark Jesus never refers to himself as the messiah or as the Son of God (with Mark 13:32 and 14:62 as possible exceptions). The narrator does, right from the beginning (1:1), and other characters do, but Jesus neither uses these titles nor affirms them. Instead, Jesus calls himself the Son of Man. Earlier in this book we have observed that Son of Man, which simply means "human" at a literal level, came to carry messianic connotations in Jewish apocalyptic literature, most notably in parts of *1 Enoch* and *4 Ezra*. Messianic thinking concerning an apocalyptic Son of Man who comes to judge the world and inaugurate an age of righteousness emerges from speculation regarding Daniel 7:13-14. There "one like a Son of Man" (literal translation) receives authority so that all nations come to serve him.

Mark clearly affirms Jesus's identity as messiah (or Christ), Son of God, and Son of Man as ways of indicating Jesus's messianic identity, but interpreters have struggled to explain why Jesus only uses "Son of Man" to refer to himself. One key problem is that interpreters are unclear as to the meaning of "Son of Man" in Daniel 7, while its occurrences in

1 Enoch (possibly) and *4 Ezra* (surely) postdate Mark's composition. In other words, in Mark Jesus uses "Son of Man" in ways that have no parallels in Jewish literature of the period.

Mark 13 includes the Gospel's most extended reflection on the Son of Man. Jesus pronounces that Jerusalem's temple will be destroyed: "not even one stone will be left upon another" (13:2), and some of his disciples ask when such things will occur and what sign will provide warning. In other words, they want to know about the culmination of history. Jesus admonishes the disciples not to be disturbed by messianic pretenders or catastrophic events—not even by persecution they will surely face. In the middle of the discourse, however, Jesus names the event that should awaken end-time expectation, the "desolating sacrilege" (13:14 NRSV; or, "abomination of desolation"). This phrase occurs in both Daniel (9:27; 11:31; 12:11) and 1 Maccabees (1:54) to indicate the profanation of Jerusalem's temple by pagans. In Mark it likely ties the coming of the Son of Man to the Romans' destruction of the Holy City and its temple. "In those days, after the suffering of that time," the Son of Man will come riding among the clouds (Mark 13:24-27).

We pause for a few comments on the use of "Son of Man" in Mark 13. First, the imagery is thoroughly apocalyptic, combining concern regarding the First Jewish Revolt (66–70 BCE) with the Son of Man's arrival. Second, Mark draws heavily upon the language of Daniel, particularly chapter 7, in which the one like a Son of Man ascends to God's throne upon the clouds of heaven and receives authority to drive out Israel's oppressors. Third, Mark's adaptation of Daniel's imagery resides not too far from its usage in *1 Enoch* and *4 Ezra*—except that Mark gives the Son of Man only one mission, to "gather together his chosen people" (Mark 13:27). Mark does not describe victory over the Romans or a final judgment, as we encounter in other texts. Finally, we observe that when Jesus describes the coming Son of Man he speaks in the third person—as if he were talking about someone else (see Mark 14:62).

Mark may discourage over-eager apocalyptic speculation, but this scenario is also designed to keep believers on their toes. Mark insists that the Son of Man's coming, or *parousia*, will happen unexpectedly. "This generation" will not have passed away before the final events take place (Mark 13:30)—a statement that has vexed interpreters through the centuries. No one knows, not even the Son, when this final scenario will play out, so believers should "watch out" and "stay alert" (13:30-35).

It is only because Jesus refers to himself as Son of Man in other contexts that we regard his language about the Son of Man's coming as self-referential. Elsewhere in Mark Jesus uses the term in two primary ways. First, he uses it to indicate his authority. The Son of Man has the authority to forgive sins (Mark 2:10), and he is lord of the Sabbath (2:28). But second, Jesus uses the term to refer to his gruesome fate. On three occasions Jesus instructs his disciples that the Son of Man "must" suffer rejection, humiliation, and execution—all before he will rise again (Mark 8:31; 9:31; 10:33-34). Mark adapts Daniel's Son of Man language to indicate Jesus's transcendent identity as the future deliverer of his people, a role that gives him authority in his own career. But "Son of Man" also indicates the peculiar shape of Jesus's messianic vocation. No one expected a messiah who would suffer and die—or be raised from the dead, for that matter—but that is precisely the kind of Son of Man/messiah Jesus represents.

Mark's Ending(s)

Modern translations of the New Testament typically include "Shorter" and "Longer" endings after Mark 16:8, usually with a footnote. The footnote indicates what we call a textual problem. Our earliest and most reliable copies of Mark all end at 16:8. Clearly later copyists, probably familiar with the endings of the other gospels, felt compelled to supply neater endings to a story that ends with women running away in fear.

Contemporary interpreters universally reject the additional endings of Mark. But is it possible that Mark's original ending has been lost? We have no direct manuscript evidence for such a possibility, but a few interpreters are convinced that Mark must originally have included such appearance stories. (See N. Clayton Croy, *The Mutilation of Mark's Gospel* [Nashville: Abingdon Press, 2003].)

Mark's story culminates, as do all the gospels, with a thoroughly apocalyptic moment. Mark's story is unique among the Gospels because it includes no appearance of the risen Jesus. The women who approach the tomb in order to tend to Jesus's body encounter not Jesus's body but a young man who informs them that Jesus is risen and will appear to them and the disciples in Galilee (Mark 16:1-7; see 14:28).

We have already encountered resurrection as a fairly new concept in Judaism, one that emerged most clearly in the literary apocalypses. Jesus's resurrection is not like the resuscitation of Jairus's daughter in chapter 5: she may have been restored to life, but she will eventually die like everyone else. Jesus's resurrection transforms his dead body into a spiritual life that will never end. The confession of Jesus's resurrection surely represented good news among early believers, but it also presented them with a serious intellectual problem. They understood resurrection as something that happened only at the end of the age, when all the righteous would receive new life. In contrast Jesus's resurrection occurs in the flow of ordinary time, and it involves only a single individual. Unlike Paul, Mark provides no detailed reflection on Jesus's resurrection. Mark does, however, prepare readers for the resurrection on multiple occasions (8:31; 9:31; 10:33-34; 14:28).

Mark's gospel begins and concludes with strong apocalyptic notes. John's baptism of repentance leads to Jesus's proclamation of the kingdom. The story features heavenly visions and heavenly voices along with Satan and the demons who recognize Jesus's identity. Jesus's victory over Satan is confirmed at the end of the story, when he rises from the dead.

Matthew: Amplifying Judgment

Matthew incorporates over ninety percent of the material from Mark's Gospel. Matthew almost always follows Mark's order, often redacting, or editing, Mark's account for strategic reasons. Matthew also adds large chunks of useful material. If we want to assess the role of apocalyptic discourse in Matthew, we must attend to those additions and modifications.

Like Mark, Matthew includes the John the Baptist story. Matthew and Luke alike present much fuller versions of Jesus's baptism and temptation narratives, along with an even more abbreviated version of Jesus's basic message: "Change your hearts and lives! Here comes the kingdom of heaven!" (Matt 4:17). (Matthew seems to prefer "kingdom of heaven" over "kingdom of God," perhaps reflecting Jewish reverence for the divine name.) We could dwell on minor details in Matthew's redaction. For example, in Mark Jesus is the one who sees the heavens rip open (Mark 1:10), but Matthew changes the story so that the heavens part for everyone to see. (In English translations the heavens open "to him," reflecting later additions to the Greek text.) Matthew also uses a less dramatic verb than does Mark (Matt 3:16). However, Matthew basically relates what Mark shares.

Nevertheless, the feel of Matthew's introduction effectively downplays the notes of apocalyptic urgency with which Mark begins. This may not be intentional. By choosing to begin with Jesus's genealogy and an infancy narrative, there's no way for Matthew to lead with John's urgent proclamation. Stylistically, Matthew eliminates almost all of Mark's breathless "and immediately" transitions. (Mark uses this device over forty times; Matthew only five.)

> ### Redaction Criticism and the Gospels
> The present discussion assumes that Matthew bases its story upon a copy of Mark. This theory, called "Marcan Priority," posits that both Matthew and Luke base their storylines on Mark and is held almost universally by biblical scholars.
>
> If Matthew is working from Mark, then Matthew must have reasons for modifying Mark's account—especially when Matthew does so with consistent tendencies. The ways in which Matthew edits Mark's story reflect the author's theological, social, and ethical outlooks. This analysis, comparing Matthew (or Luke) to Mark and drawing conclusions from Matthew's editing (or redaction) of Mark, is called redaction criticism.

Other signs suggest, however, that Matthew is working to slow down Mark's urgent expectation. Mark's hurried introduction moves from Jesus's initial proclamation (Mark 1:14-15) to the calling of the disciples. Then Jesus performs his first powerful deed—while teaching in a synagogue, he carries out an exorcism (1:21-28). Teaching, healing, and exorcism define Jesus's ministry as Mark presents it (1:32-34, 38-39). To this pattern Matthew offers some subtle changes. Immediately following the calling of Peter, Andrew, James, and John—the point at which Mark presents Jesus's first exorcism—Matthew substitutes a summary of Jesus's ministry. This summary effectively demotes Jesus's encounters with demons.

> Jesus traveled throughout Galilee, teaching in their synagogues. He announced the good news of the kingdom and healed every disease and sickness among the people. News about him spread throughout all Syria. People brought to him all those who had various kinds of diseases, those in pain, those *possessed by demons*, those with epilepsy, and those who were paralyzed, and he healed them. Large crowds followed him from Galilee, the Decapolis, Jerusalem, Judea, and from the areas beyond the Jordan River. (Matt 4:23-25, emphasis added)

Matthew follows this scene with the Sermon on the Mount, the most prominent block of Jesus's teaching material in the Gospels (chaps. 5–7). The Sermon certainly includes some apocalyptic motifs. It includes a final judgment (7:21-23) and a Gehenna (CEB: "hell") of fire (5:22; see 7:19). Matthew's famous beatitudes ("Blessed are…") anticipate a final state in which present injustices will be reversed. On the whole, however, the Sermon on the Mount disrupts the note of expectation and conflict we encounter in Mark's story by foregrounding Jesus's identity as an authoritative teacher. And that first exorcism in Mark 1:21-28? Matthew eliminates that story entirely. Whatever the reason, Matthew's introduction significantly softens the impression of apocalyptic expectation we find in Mark.

Gehenna

In the Synoptic Gospels Jesus sometimes refers to Gehenna, associating it with fiery judgment. Luke employs the term only once, Mark three times in one passage, but Matthew seven times in five passages. James 3:6 suggests that the tongue, a dangerous weapon, is set on fire by Gehenna. Other ancient Jewish literature also employs Gehenna as a place of punishment. Some modern translations render Gehenna as "hell," but the word *Gehenna* derives from a Hebrew term that simply means "Valley of Hinnom."

It's often said that Jesus and others refer to Gehenna because it was a trash dump outside Jerusalem that often smoldered or because it had been a place of child sacrifice according to the Hebrew Bible (see Jer 7:30-34; 19:1-13).[4] No one knows for sure why Gehenna came to have this connotation or how ancient readers of the Gospels understood it.[5]

The Synoptic Take(s) on Jesus

In other respects Matthew amplifies Mark's apocalyptic emphases. Mark does reference judgment, but rarely. In one passage Mark warns of the Gehenna of fire (Mark 9:43-47), and the parable of the tenants implies judgment against the temple authorities (12:1-12; see 12:40), but generally Mark does not dwell on the topic. But judgment language is definitely big for Matthew—and in surprising ways.

Matthew is especially fond of final judgment imagery, far more than is Mark. Matthew shares some sayings (Q material) with Luke. "The ax is already at the root of the trees" (Matt 3:10; Luke 3:9). Where Mark reads, "he will baptize you with the Holy Spirit" (Mark 1:8), Matthew has "he will baptize you with the Holy Spirit and with fire" (Matt 3:11; Luke 3:16). In fact, Matthew includes two other references to fire in the John the Baptist account (3:10, 12), along with a warning about "the angry judgment that is coming" (3:7; Luke 3:7). The same language occurs in Luke, suggesting that it derives from Q material rather than from Matthew's redaction of Mark.

However, the fire-and-judgment language fits Matthew particularly well. One of Matthew's distinctive parables, the parable of the weeds and its explanation (Matt 13:24-30, 36-43), alludes to a furnace of fire for all who do evil. While "the righteous will shine like the sun," the wicked will weep and gnash their teeth (13:42-43). As with fire imagery, Matthew also delights in the imagery of weeping and grinding of teeth, which never occurs in Mark and appears only once in Luke (13:28). Matthew uses this striking word picture six times (Matt 8:12; 13:42, 50; 22:13; 24:51; 25:30).

Matthew's emphasis on a final judgment manifests itself most clearly in a set of parables characterized by explicit imagery. Like Mark 4, Matthew 13 is devoted to parables and begins with the parable of the sower and its explanation, followed by "The kingdom of heaven is like" parables. Matthew adds two parables that clearly envision a final judgment, the parable of the weeds among the wheat and its explanation (13:24-30, 36-43) and the parable of the net (13:47-50). Both parables occur only in Matthew, and both employ the imagery of fire and the gnashing of teeth.

Matthew shares the parable of the feast (22:1-14) with Luke (14:15-24) and the Gospel of Thomas (64). Matthew, however, adds a striking, even bizarre twist to the story. When the host (a king in Matthew) encounters a guest who lacks a wedding garment, the poor guest is bound and tossed into the outer darkness, where people weep and grind their teeth. The perplexing thing about this detail is that the poor guest has been brought in only at the last moment. Is it fair to condemn him for failing to find a change of clothes?

The parable of the ten virgins occurs only in Matthew (25:1-13), and it too involves end-time imagery. Five make it into the feast, and five find themselves left in the cold. Also built around a wedding feast, this parable includes language Jesus elsewhere applies to the final judgment: "I don't know you" (Matt 25:12; see 7:21-23). It also echoes Jesus's language about the coming (*parousia*) of the Son of Man: "you don't know the day or the hour" (Matt 25:13; see 24:36).

Matthew's next parable, the talents (25:14-30), basically echoes Luke's parable of the pounds (Luke 19:12-27). Again Matthew features judgment details lacking in Luke. The poor slave who buries the lord's treasure finds himself—guess where?—in the outer darkness, where people weep and grind their teeth.

The famous parable of the sheep and the goats occurs only in Matthew (25:31-46) and follows the parable of the talents. It begins with the Son of Man sitting on a throne, dividing the peoples as one separates sheep from goats. The separation motif recalls the parables of the weeds and the wheat and the net from chapter 13. The sorting results in some going away to eternal punishment and others to eternal life.

So Matthew includes lots of judgment imagery, especially among parables that occur only in Matthew or in details that appear only in Matthew's versions. But Matthew's understanding of judgment comes with a twist. Folks don't really know which side they're on until after judgment happens. For example, not everyone who calls Jesus "Lord" will enter the kingdom of heaven (7:21-23). The underdressed wedding guest has no reason to expect he should dress up, and the five unfortunate virgins are "foolish" only because they do not anticipate the bridegroom's delay or their peers' selfishness. (After all, couldn't the bridesmaids just light one lamp at a time, sharing oil until the bridegroom's arrival?) Goats don't know they're goats until it's too late. The fortunate sheep find themselves no less surprised! In Matthew's world judgment is precarious business.

Since all four gospels include resurrection scenes, with only Mark lacking appearances of the risen Jesus, we won't review the phenomenon of resurrection in each one. But Matthew's version of Jesus's crucifixion includes a remarkable detail. An earthquake occurs at the moment of Jesus's death, opening the tombs in Jerusalem. In perhaps the Bible's creepiest moment, "many" bodies of holy people are raised from their tombs—Matthew uses one of the New Testament's two words of resurrection here—and wander around Jerusalem. What becomes of these resurrected saints, Matthew does not speculate (27:51-54).[6]

Like Mark, Matthew and Luke include Jesus's discourse concerning the temple's destruction and the Son of Man. This speech occurs in Matthew 24, and Matthew specifies the disciples' key question: they want to know, "What will be the sign of your coming [*parousia*] and the end of the age?" (24:3) To Mark's account Matthew adds concern about the "nations" (CEB), indicating Matthew's interest in a mission among Gentiles. (The Greek word *ethnoi* may refer to nations in the abstract or to Gentiles, the "nations," from a Jewish perspective.) The disciples will be hated by "all nations," and the end will come only after the gospel has been proclaimed among the nations (24:9, 14).

Matthew also adds the concept of an end-time apostasy, a fragmentation among the faithful (24:10-13). The concept of end-time crisis amounts to an apocalyptic commonplace, with a specific expectation that some of the faithful may fall into apostasy—a variation on that theme. We have seen this topic in letters attributed to Paul like 2 Thessalonians (2:3) and 1 Timothy (4:1). Matthew envisions "many" falling away and betraying one another under the threat of persecution. True believers must endure to the end (Matt 24:10-13).

In conclusion, while Matthew adopts Mark's eschatological emphases, it just slightly moderates Mark's note of immediacy. On the other hand,

Matthew devotes far more extensive reflection to the question of a final judgment and the uncertainty that attends it.

Luke: Toning Down Expectations

Luke shares the general apocalyptic expectations of Mark and Matthew, but Luke tends to downplay the sense of imminent expectation while adding a sense of the kingdom's presence in the here and now. According to a common view, Mark was composed during or just after the First Jewish Revolt, a crisis that aroused hope that Jesus's return might occur at any moment. We recall that Paul himself had expected to be alive at the *parousia*. Luke, writing at a later period, does not share this sense of eschatological urgency, after two or three generations have passed on. According to this view, Luke is concerned more with discipleship for the long haul than with breathless anticipation. This common view holds some truth, but most interpreters today find it lacking. Luke does not so much *discourage* eschatological hope as Luke *reinterprets* it.

Luke deals with eschatological matters and apocalyptic *topoi* in complicated, even inconsistent ways. Like Matthew, Luke leads with stories about Jesus's infancy before introducing John the Baptist (Luke 3:1-22). As in Matthew (Q material) "the ax is already at the root of the trees" (Luke 3:9). Moreover, the coming one "will baptize you with the Holy Spirit and fire," and "he will bring the wheat into his barn" but burn the chaff "with a fire that can't be put out" (Luke 3:16-17). Luke inserts Jesus's genealogy between John's appearance and Jesus's temptation, softening the sense of eschatological urgency, but the apocalyptic elements remain: after Jesus's baptism the heavens part and a heavenly voice announces Jesus's identity (Luke 3:21-22), while Jesus's temptation includes a direct confrontation with the devil (4:1-13; Q material again). Luke eliminates the note of repentance and the nearness of the kingdom from the summary of Jesus's ministry (4:14-15; see Mark 1:14-15). In short, Luke maintains some of the apocalyptic and eschatological material but mutes the element of imminence. Asked when the kingdom of God will arrive, Jesus replies that the kingdom is "*among* you" now (Luke 17:20-21, emphasis added).

Thus, Luke goes for a different kind of imminence. Jesus brings salvation *now*. Luke is more fond of salvation language, including the verb *to save* (*sōzō*) and the term *Savior*, than are Matthew and Mark. Luke, but not Matthew or Mark, identifies Jesus as savior. Jesus uses the language of salvation when he announces someone's forgiveness (Luke 7:50; 19:9). The same language applies to both healings (Luke 6:9; 8:48; 17:19) and exorcisms (8:36).

Luke does not eliminate future expectation, but the Gospel does tend to stress salvation's arrival in the person of Jesus rather than at some future point. The first of Jesus's public appearances provides a case in point. Mark and Matthew narrate Jesus's unsuccessful teaching session in his hometown synagogue (Mark 6:1-6a; Matt 13:53-58). Those stories occur just about in the middle of Mark and Matthew, but Luke advances the scene to the very beginning of Jesus's ministry (4:16-30). There it functions much like the Sermon on the Mount in Matthew: as an introduction to the content of Jesus's ministry.

Jesus reads from two passages in Isaiah—Luke presents them as if they were a single passage. He claims the Holy Spirit has come upon him, a message that carries eschatological freight. John the Baptist has already linked Jesus with the arrival of the Holy Spirit and of fire (Luke 3:16). The same author composed both Luke and Acts; quoting Joel, the very first speech in Acts envisions an end-time outpouring of the Spirit (Acts 2:17-18; Joel 2:28-32). So Jesus's claim that the Holy Spirit has come upon him, buttressed by his reference to "the year of the Lord's favor" (Luke 4:18-19), identifies his ministry as an eschatological event. But this event occurs right in the here and now, not in some remote future. It takes place in the good news Jesus offers to the poor, to captives, to the blind, and to the oppressed.

Early Jews and Christians held diverse views concerning the afterlife.[7] Among the Gospels Luke stands out for its view on the topic. Mark does not speculate on the question, but we have seen Matthew's interest in a final judgment. Matthew also features the scene in which the bodies of the dead rise from their graves at the moment of Jesus's death (Matt 27:51-53). These two items, the final judgment and the rising of the saints at Jesus's death, are consistent with the view that the dead remain just that—dead—until a final judgment. John's Gospel, by the way, yields the same impression by referring to a final resurrection: "the time is coming," Jesus says, "when all who are in their graves" will rise for judgment (John 5:28-29; see 11:24).

Two passages in Luke suggest a very different view: when people die, they go immediately to their ultimate fate. The first case appears in the parable of the rich man and Lazarus (Luke 16:19-31). Upon his death the angels carry Lazarus to Abraham's bosom, but the rich man finds himself tormented in Hades. We may go too far to assume that a parable conveys Jesus's—or Luke's—views on an item such as the afterlife: the parables are instructive fictions, after all, and perhaps this parable is simply drawing upon stock imagery to make a larger point. However, Luke and only Luke relates Jesus's promise to one of the criminals crucified alongside him: "today you will be with me in Paradise" (23:43).

Like the "Little Apocalypses" of Mark 13 and Matthew 24, Luke 21:5-38 begins with Jesus's announcement of the temple's destruction and the question from his disciples, "Teacher, when will these things happen? What sign will show that these things are about to happen?" (Luke 21:7). Luke redacts Mark's account subtly but to great effect.[8]

- Mark's Jesus warns that "Many people will come in my name, saying, 'I'm the one!'" (Mark 13:6). To this admonition Luke adds, "Many will come in my name, saying, 'I'm the one!' and, 'It's time!'" (Luke 21:8). Those who claim the end is at hand are just as dangerous as are false messiahs.

- Luke 21:9 also edits Mark 13:7. In Mark 13:7, Jesus informs the disciples that "this isn't the end yet." Luke redacts this to, "the end won't happen immediately" (21:9).

- Mark 13:8 interprets wars, earthquakes, and famines as signs of the end: "These things are just the beginning of the sufferings associated with the end." Luke 21:10-11 mentions the portents, but downplays Mark's urgent timing by eliminating the references to the beginning of sufferings and to the end.

- Following Mark, Luke depicts the siege of Jerusalem as a time of great suffering. In Mark God intervenes to "cut short" this period (Mark 13:20). Luke omits any reference to divine intervention here and introduces an indefinite period: "Jerusalem will be plundered by Gentiles until the times of the Gentiles are concluded" (21:24).

- Like Mark, Luke refers to the Son of Man's arrival "with power and great splendor" (Luke 21:27). But Luke adds that only then—when the Son of Man returns, not when catastrophes ravage the earth—Jesus's followers will know that their redemption has drawn near (21:28).

> **M Material and L Material**
>
> Matthew and Luke alike build their stories on Mark's narrative. They also include what we call Q material, defined as content that occurs in Matthew and Luke but not Mark. Matthew and Luke also contain unique content of their own, known as M material (for Matthew) and L material (for Luke). M and L material may derive from previous literary sources or may derive from the authors' own creative contributions.

- Luke concludes the Little Apocalypse with L material, content we find only in Luke (21:34-36). Luke insists that disciples remain alert, for "that day" will arrive suddenly. Moreover, they must not allow debauchery or drunkenness to weigh them down. Perhaps Luke fears that moral discipline will falter with the *parousia*'s delay? The passage concludes with concern regarding ordinary distractions (CEB: "the anxieties of day-to-day life"; see 8:14). Luke has repeatedly shown how ordinary concerns can hinder people from Jesus's urgent demand to follow him (Luke 9:57-62; 14:15-24). In other words, Luke calls for urgency in the here and now, with awareness that Jesus could return at any moment.

Luke is walking the tightrope. Luke discourages people from expecting the kingdom of God to break in right away (19:11). But of course the Son of Man's advent will be sudden, as fast as lightning flashing across the sky (17:24). Luke encourages eschatological readiness, but without speculation concerning the timing of Jesus's return.

Any consideration of Luke must also take account of the book of Acts. The same person composed both works: on this all interpreters agree. Opinions vary, however, regarding how Luke's Gospel and Acts relate to one another. Some regard the two books as a single work in two volumes. These tend to discuss Luke–Acts as a literary unity. Others, including myself, see Acts as a sort of sequel to Luke, perhaps composed years later. We can leave this debate to other books. Our attention lies with apocalyptic discourse and its contribution to Acts.

Acts does not tend to focus upon apocalyptic topics. However, Jesus's resurrection and identity as Israel's messiah provide the core of Acts's gospel message, and his return as judge plays a role nearly as central (e.g., Acts 2:22-36; 3:18-26; 10:34-43; 26:19-23).

Acts's interpretation of history depends heavily upon the apocalyptic narrative and proves fundamental to the book's plot. Many interpreters identify Acts 1:8 as a sort of thesis statement for the whole book: once the Holy Spirit empowers Jesus's followers, they will spread the gospel around the world. This theme implies a sort of end to history: good news to all people fulfills the trajectory of God's covenant with Abraham (Gen 12:1-3; Isa 66:18-24). When the Holy Spirit does fall upon the disciples, Peter interprets it as the dawn of a new age.

> *In the last days*, God says,
> I will pour out my Spirit on all people.
>   Your sons and daughters will prophesy.
>   Your young will see visions.
>   Your elders will dream dreams.
> Even upon my servants, men and women,
>   I will pour out my Spirit in those days, and they will prophesy.
> I will cause wonders to occur in the heavens above
>   and signs on the earth below,
>   blood and fire and a cloud of smoke.
> The sun will be changed into darkness,

      and the moon will be changed into blood,
        before the great and spectacular day of the Lord comes.
And *everyone who calls on the name of the Lord will be saved.*
(Acts 2:17-21; quoting Joel 2:28-32)

Acts emphasizes that Jesus's resurrection inaugurates "these days" (3:24; 13:38-41), in which the gospel is proclaimed around the world. By the end of the story, the gospel has reached all the way to Rome.

Acts draws upon apocalyptic discourse in another particularly significant way. As we have seen in other sections, apocalyptic discourse can lend authority to a speaker or to a theological perspective. A revelation received directly from God merits special attention. As in several of Paul's letters, the crucial debate in Acts involves the incorporation of non-Jews, or Gentiles, into the people of God. Judaism openly welcomed converts, but the New Testament has in view Gentiles who devote themselves to Jesus without converting to Judaism; that is, without taking on the obligations of diet, Sabbath, and circumcision. Jesus apparently left no clear instruction regarding this possibility, nor do the Jewish Scriptures address it clearly.

Acts favors the incorporation of Gentiles into the churches apart from conversion to Judaism, and it uses apocalyptic discourse to make the point. In chapter 9 Saul, soon to be renamed Paul, experiences a dramatic encounter with the risen Jesus while he is on a mission to persecute Christians in Damascus. Blinded by brilliant light, Paul hears Jesus's voice command him to enter Damascus. He neither eats nor drinks for three days. Meanwhile, a believer in Damascus named Ananias has a vision of his own. Ananias is to go to Paul, lay hands on him, and restore his sight. When Ananias expresses reluctance regarding this mission, he learns its larger purpose: Paul will bring Jesus's name before Gentiles and Jews alike. As Acts develops, Paul becomes the foremost missionary to the Gentiles.

Very soon Peter receives a vision of his own. Praying on a rooftop in Joppa, and hungry because he has not eaten, Peter sees a sheet descend from heaven, carrying all kinds of animals Jews are not permitted to eat. "Get up, Peter! Kill and eat" (Acts 10:13). Three times Peter hears this message reinforced: "Never consider unclean what God has made pure" (10:15). Like Paul's vision, Peter's has a counterpart: a Roman centurion named Cornelius has already experienced a vision of his own, leading him to send for Peter. The men are approaching even while Peter prays (10:1-9). These two visions lead Peter to preach the gospel to Cornelius and his household, not only leading to their conversion but winning the approval of the other apostles in Jerusalem.

The visions of Paul and Peter legitimate the mission to the Gentiles. Several factors link these visions together. First, both visions involve the inclusion of Gentiles, and Acts places them very close together—consecutive chapters in modern Bibles. Second, each vision is confirmed by a corresponding vision: one by Ananias and the other by Cornelius. And third, each vision is narrated thrice. Paul summarizes his experience in Acts 22:6-11 and 26:12-20, while Peter repeats his in Acts 11:5-14 and 15:7-9. Not only does Acts present a gospel message with a heavy apocalyptic inflection, it authorizes that message by means of apocalyptic visions.

Conclusion

Thoroughly apocalyptic, Mark's storyline shapes the narratives of both Matthew and Luke. The apocalyptic preacher John baptizes Jesus in the Jordan River. Then Jesus experiences an apocalyptic revelation, in which the skies part and a heavenly voice reveals his identity as God's Son. Immediately Jesus endures temptation by the devil in the wilderness. Upon his return to society Jesus calls people to repent because God's kingdom has drawn near. Throughout the story but particularly in the beginning, Jesus demonstrates his authority in the spirit realm by casting out demons. Jesus teaches about the coming Son of Man, particularly in a lengthy apocalyptic discourse that prepares disciples for the last days. As conflict escalates Jesus informs his disciples—not once but three times—that he will be executed, then raised from the dead. This story, in which God's Son comes to earth to overcome demonic forces, is to all appearances defeated through his crucifixion, and yet is raised from the dead by the power of God, entirely depends on apocalyptic categories.

Matthew and Luke follow Mark's storyline, but each Gospel inflects the apocalyptic bits differently. Matthew tends to soften Mark's stress upon the nearness of Jesus's return, but Matthew intensifies the theme of a final judgment that separates the righteous from the wicked. Luke encourages believers to be prepared for Jesus's return but tends to interpret that readiness in terms of daily faithfulness rather than end-time speculation. Luke's distinctiveness comes through perhaps most strongly in the composition of Acts: there Jesus's followers interpret his resurrection and the age of the Spirit as inaugurating the last days. Visions authenticate Luke's message of Gentile inclusion, but the focus lies not with the end of history but with spreading the gospel in the here and now. Matthew and Luke differ in another respect: Matthew describes an end-time resurrection of the dead, whereas Luke apparently assumes that people go to their eternal destinies upon their deaths.

A major question yet remains: how do the Synoptic portraits relate to Jesus himself? Did Jesus conform to the apocalyptic narrative established by Mark and largely followed by Matthew and Luke? Most historians who take up the question of the historical Jesus regard the Synoptics as our most valuable sources for imagining who Jesus was and what he was about. Before we address the question of Jesus, however, we should consider other early interpretations of him. These include the hypothetical collection of sayings attributed to Jesus called Q and the Gospels of John and Thomas.

For Further Reading

Bauckham, Richard. *The Fate of the Dead: Studies on the Jewish and Christian Apocalypses.* NovTSup 93. Leiden: Brill, 1998.

Blount, Brian K. *Go Preach! Mark's Kingdom Message and the Black Church Today.* Maryknoll, NY: Orbis Books, 2000.

Boring, M. Eugene. *Mark: A Commentary.* Old Testament Library. Louisville: Westminster John Knox Press, 2006.

Carey, Greg. *The Gospel According to Luke: All Flesh Shall See God's Salvation.* Phoenix Guides to the New Testament. Sheffield, England: Phoenix, 2012.

Carter, Warren. *Matthew: Storyteller, Interpreter, Evangelist.* Peabody, MA: Hendrickson, 2004.

Clark-Soles, Jaime. *Death and the Afterlife in the New Testament*. New York: T and T Clark, 2006.

Green, Joel B. *The Gospel of Luke*. The New International Commentary on the New Testament. Grand Rapids: Eerdmans, 1997.

Levison, John R. "Holy Spirit." Pages 2.859–79 in *NIDB*. Nashville: Abingdon Press, 2007.

Myers, Ched. *Binding the Strong Man: A Political Reading of Mark's Story of Jesus*. Maryknoll, NY: Orbis Books, 1992.

Nelson, Richard D. "Tribes, Territories of." *NIDB* 6.668–76.

Chapter Five
Beyond the Synoptic Gospels: Q, Thomas, John—and Jesus

Not all gospels share Mark's basic storyline. Mark begins with John the Baptist and his message of imminent repentance, introduces Jesus through a visionary experience that occurs at his baptism, demonstrates his identity and power by showing him overcome temptation in the wilderness, and inaugurates his ministry with the proclamation that the time is near and the kingdom of God lies at hand. Matthew and Luke generally follow along, altering Mark's account to bring forth their own emphases. Three other gospels—one hypothetical, one canonical, and a third perhaps quite ancient—portray Jesus differently. The Q source, a hypothetical document containing material common to Matthew and Luke but absent from Mark, contains a good deal of apocalyptic material but elaborates Jesus's teachings rather than following Mark's narrative arc. John's Gospel begins not with John the Baptist but beyond history: "In the beginning was the Word...." The Gospel of Thomas may or may not reflect first-century traditions about Jesus, but it rejects all forms of apocalyptic and eschatological speculation.

We have a Synoptic storyline that is thoroughly apocalyptic in both plot and emphasis countered by the diverse orientations of Q, John, and Thomas. All of these sources revolve around the figure of Jesus. This diversity leads us to ask how much we can know about Jesus and his relationship to apocalyptic discourse.

The Matter of Q

Matthew and Luke each draw much of their material from Mark's Gospel, but they also share a substantial amount of material that Mark lacks, 225–250 verses depending on who's counting. To explain this phenomenon, scholars proposed a hypothetical document, Q, from which the authors of Matthew and Luke both drew. While Matthew and Luke generally follow Mark's storyline, they do not use Q in the same way: Q material shows up in diverse locations in these two gospels. Yet the strong amount of shared material with remarkably similar wording, along with the particular ways in which it appears in Matthew and Luke, has satisfied most interpreters that those two gospels must have shared a second literary source.[1]

> **Citing Q**
> Students often find confusing the chapter and verse numbers assigned to Q in scholarly literature. Because many scholars believe Luke renders Q more conservatively than does Matthew, these references point to a passage's location in Luke. In other words, we find Q 11:14-23 at Luke 11:14-23.

Q contains quite a bit of eschatological material, including apocalyptic topics. As we have seen, Q provides much fuller accounts of John the Baptist and of Jesus's temptation than does Mark, and the Q versions amplify the apocalyptic tones of both scenes. John the Baptist threatens judgment. "The ax is already at the root of the trees"; bad trees and chaff will be cut down and thrown into the fire. And where Mark's Jesus will baptize you with the Holy Spirit, in Q he baptizes "with the Holy Spirit and fire." Much longer than Mark's, Q's temptation account develops *how* the devil tests Jesus, offering him a series of opportunities to glorify himself.

Several apocalyptic topics appear here and there in Q, but rarely do we find concentrated doses of any. Q shows little interest in Jesus's death or in his resurrection. It calls disciples to take up their crosses (Luke 14:27;

Matt 10:38), but it does not dwell specifically on Jesus's own cross.[2] Nor does Q say anything directly of Jesus's resurrection, although some Q passages presuppose a final resurrection and judgment (Luke 11:31-32; see Matt 12:42).[3]

Q does include exorcisms and the accusation that Jesus casts out demons because he is in league with the devil, Beelzebul (Luke 11:14-23; Matt 12:22-30). Q also features Jesus's warning concerning how "this generation" seeks a sign but will receive only "Jonah's sign" (11:29-32; Matt 12:38-42). Perhaps this sign refers simply to Jonah's prophetic ministry to Nineveh, but it may well also point to Jesus's resurrection: just as Jonah was miraculously delivered from death, so will Jesus be.[4] Furthermore, Jesus's saying about this generation presupposes a final judgment: "The people of Nineveh will rise up at the judgment with this generation and condemn it," a view also reflected in Luke 10:13-15 and Matthew 11:21-23. Q expresses the expectation of the Son of Man's unexpected *parousia* (Luke 17:27-37; Matt 24:26-28, 40-41), along with some interest in the afterlife (Luke 12:4-5 and 13:28-29; Matt 10:28 and 8:11-12). Q presents the Son of Man's coming as an abrupt surprise.

One Q passage holds particular interest.

Matthew 19:28	Luke 22:28-30
Jesus said to them, "I assure you who have followed me that, when everything is made new, when the Human One sits on his magnificent throne, you also will sit on twelve thrones overseeing the twelve tribes of Israel. And all who have left houses, brothers, sisters, father, mother, children, or farms because of my name will receive a hundred times more and will inherit eternal life."	[Jesus said,] "You are the ones who have continued with me in my trials. And I confer royal power on you just as my Father granted royal power to me. Thus you will eat and drink at my table in my kingdom, and you will sit on thrones overseeing the twelve tribes of Israel."

Jesus's promise that his disciples will occupy twelve thrones, judging (CEB: "overseeing") Israel's twelve tribes, reflects an apocalyptic hope. The Assyrian conquest of the Northern Kingdom in 722/721 BCE effectively eliminated ten of Israel's twelve tribes, at least in the popular imagination. For God to reconstitute all of Israel's twelve tribes would require an eschatological miracle—and that's just what this passage has in mind (see Ezek 47:13–48:35).[5] The book of Revelation symbolically reflects this hope and links the twelve tribes with the twelve apostles (Rev 7:4-8; 21:12-14). Moreover, the exaltation of the twelve accompanies the Son of Man's arrival. This expectation may go back to Jesus himself, as we see it also reflected in the request of James and John to receive prominent places when Jesus comes in glory (Mark 10:37; Matt 20:21).

Interpreters have devoted a lot of attention to the presence of apocalyptic topics in Q. John S. Kloppenborg, among others, famously proposed that Q developed over time. Q's earliest layer would not have included apocalyptic and eschatological concerns: those emerged later. This core layer offered wisdom for comportment and mission in the world. Later "prophetic" sayings were added, including the material about judgment and the coming Son of Man.[6] Kloppenborg's proposal proved influential in debates concerning Jesus and his message, a topic we'll take up later. Q's first layer would amount to our earliest collection of Jesus's sayings. If it lacks apocalyptic material, then perhaps Jesus did not address topics like demons and their activities, a final judgment, the coming of the Son of Man. And perhaps Mark's Gospel gets Jesus totally wrong.

> **Layering Q**
> Is it possible to identify a history of development within Q, separating earlier from later levels? Many interpreters find such attempts misguided. After all, Q is a hypothetical document. No copies of it actually exist. Even if its existence is highly likely, how do we know what it looked like? What if Matthew and Luke used only parts of it and we lack access to others?

Many interpreters express skepticism that we can identify discrete layers of development within Q. It is a hypothetical document, after all. Some find it highly questionable to perform source and redaction analysis on a document we don't even have and for which we have no point of comparison. Moreover, if Q did exist, we cannot know the entirety of its contents. (Some Q experts, however, believe we have good reason to think Matthew and Luke preserved almost all of Q.) Even more interesting, some have proposed precisely the opposite sequence of Kloppenborg's proposal and believe that Q's apocalyptic material emerged earliest. Still others say that while Q's apocalyptic material may have emerged at a later stage, it may still reflect authentic Jesus tradition. As it stands, however, Q devotes significant attention to apocalyptic topics.

Reversal constitutes one intriguing aspect of Q's apocalyptic outlook—and perhaps even of the Jesus movement as a whole. In one enigmatic statement, Jesus warns his audience of the "weeping and grinding of teeth" that will occur when *you* see the patriarchs and prophets in the kingdom and *you yourselves* cast out. After all, "those who are last will be first and those who are first will be last" (Luke 13:28-30; see Matt 8:11-12; 19:30; 20:16). Matthew's version of the Beatitudes ("Blessed are..."; 5:1-12) is more famous than Luke's (6:20-26), but both presuppose a reversal of status. Matthew may bless the "poor in spirit" (5:3 NRSV) while Luke blesses the actual poor. Indeed, Luke's Jesus blesses the poor and explicitly pronounces woe upon the rich (6:20, 24). In both cases, however, the poor receive the kingdom of God.

John and Thomas

Beyond the Synoptic Gospels and the Q material contained in Matthew and Luke, two other early gospels develop their own distinctive approaches to apocalyptic discourse. John's Gospel incorporates apocalyptic motifs but tends to downplay attention to expectations regarding Jesus's return and a final judgment along with attention to the devil and his supernatural allies. The Gospel of Thomas explicitly rejects apocalyptic speculation. To complicate matters, some interpreters perceive a relationship between John and Thomas, in which John offers a critical response to Thomas.

Interpreters routinely distinguish between John and the Synoptic Gospels. Apart from Jesus's trial, execution, and resurrection, John shares little material with the other canonical Gospels. Thematically, John stands apart from the Synoptics in significant ways.

- In the Synoptics Jesus speaks continually about the kingdom of God and rarely about his own messianic identity. In John Jesus's favorite subject is, well, Jesus. Not only does Jesus affirm his messianic identity throughout John, so do other participants in the story.

- In John Jesus does not deliver the distinctive parables we encounter in the Synoptic tradition.

- In the Synoptics the adult Jesus visits Jerusalem only once, the visit that leads to his death. John reports multiple trips to and from Jerusalem.

- John's Jesus provides almost no straightforward ethical instruction, as do the Synoptics. John certainly has no material to compare with the ethical teaching from Matthew's Sermon on the Mount or Luke's Sermon on the Plain. And while the Synoptic Jesus exhorts disciples to love their neighbors or even love their enemies (Matt 5:43-47; Luke 6:27-35), John's Jesus instructs them to "love one another" (John 13:34-35; 15:12-17).

- John features no extended discourse on the last days, a final judgment, or the *parousia* such as we see in Mark 13, Matthew 24–25, and Luke 21.

Despite John's distinctiveness from the Synoptic tradition, John affirms quite a few of the distinctively apocalyptic motifs we find in the other canonical Gospels. We have seen that messianic speculation crystalized within apocalyptic literature and that Matthew, Mark, and Luke alike affirm Jesus's identity as messiah, Son of God, and Son of Man. If anything, John foregrounds Jesus's messianic identity more intensely. Jesus explicitly identifies himself as the messiah within John's story (4:25-26), as do quite a few other characters. According to John, those who confess Jesus as messiah are subject to expulsion from the synagogues—and this within Jesus's lifetime (9:22; see 16:2).

As for other apocalyptic topics, the general picture with John is somewhat complicated, affirming some apocalyptic concepts but in ways that may diminish their importance. For example, John directly refers to the devil or Satan on only three occasions, having Jesus tell disputants in an argument they are the devil's children and attributing Judas's betrayal of Jesus to the devil's influence (John 8:44; 13:2, 27). Never does Jesus perform exorcisms, as he does so often in the Synoptic Gospels, nor do we see demons blamed for human problems. Instead, Jesus's opponents accuse him of being demon-possessed (John 7:20; 8:48-52; 10:20-21). John somewhat downplays the language of the demonic in comparison with the Synoptics, but John also acknowledges that Jesus has "thrown out" and judged "this world's ruler" (12:31; 16:11). What remains unclear is whether this supernatural adversary still exerts his maleficent influence during the period after Jesus's death.

To take another example, John's Gospel is full of judgment language (e.g., 3:19; 5:22-30; 9:39), but it never speculates concerning a final judgment. John features no final judgment imagery, no weeping and gnashing of teeth, no fire (unless one counts John 15:6), no sheep and goats. John the Baptist never warns people to repent in view of the coming kingdom, nor does he promise that Jesus will baptize with fire. John's Gospel never provides any of the imagery we typically associate with hell. Some of the judgment language relates to John's presentation of Jesus's life as a sort of trial. People "seek" Jesus and try to arrest him. Jesus repeatedly discusses the "testimony" that demonstrates his true identity.[7] In some ways, then, it is almost as if people judge themselves through their responses to Jesus (John 3:17-21; 5:24; 12:48). Ultimately, however, some things remain unclear. For example, does judgment occur in the here and now, in people's immediate response to Jesus (John 5:24), or does judgment also involve a final judgment after the resurrection of the dead (5:28-30)? It is also unclear who does the judging from John's point of view: has the Father entrusted all judgment to the Son (5:22-27), or does the Father reserve judgment for himself (8:50)? After all, those who disobey the Son face God's wrath (John 3:36).

Another confusing element in John involves the relationship between resurrection and eternal life. At points John clearly asserts that those who believe in Jesus have already received eternal life (3:36; 4:14). But John also points forward to a future resurrection (5:21). Some passages even blend both motifs: one who believes in Jesus has life now, but on the last day the dead who hear the Son's voice will live (John 5:24-30; 6:47-54).

Some interpreters describe John as having a "realized" eschatology, in which believers have already received salvation in its fullness. That view was more common a few decades ago than it is now. Today, most interpreters would group John's view among the "inaugurated" eschatologies we have found in Paul and the Synoptics. If John is consistent, something we should not take for granted, it teaches that believers receive life from Jesus in the present *and* will be raised to a new life on the last day. Perhaps from John's point of view Jesus has already defeated "this world's ruler" in a fundamental sense, but the devil continues to resist until the last day.

In contrast to John, the Gospel of Thomas totally rejects apocalyptic questions and categories. This conclusion stands in contrast to those interpreters who regard John and Thomas as sharing realized eschatologies, and it is significant because Thomas, like John, posits that readers may receive life in the present and never taste death.

Whoever finds the interpretation of these sayings will not taste death. (Gos. Thom. 1, trans. Ehrman and Pleše)	[Jesus said,] "I assure you that whoever keeps my word will never die." (John 8:51)
	Jesus said to her, "I am the resurrection and the life. Whoever believes in me will live, even though they die. Everyone who lives and believes in me will never die. Do you believe this?" (John 11:25-26)

Taken together, the passages in John are somewhat ambiguous. Both passages propose that believers in Jesus will never die. But John 11:25-26 acknowledges that believers do not escape death, although they live. This apparent ambiguity reflects John's inaugurated eschatology. Thomas suffers from no such ambiguity. Those who understand Jesus's "secret" sayings transcend death right away.

> ### Thomas and the Canonical Gospels
> In 1945 the Gospel of Thomas was discovered among the other works known at the Nag Hammadi Library. All of those manuscripts date to the fourth century, long after the canonical Gospels were composed. However, references to a Gospel of Thomas go back to the early third century, and fragments of the gospel exist that date to about 200 CE. It is possible, then, that Thomas was composed quite early.
>
> Many of the sayings in Thomas overlap substantially with passages from the canonical Gospels. Interpreters debate whether the Gospel of Thomas depends on the canonical Gospels for this material or derives from its own independent streams of Jesus tradition. While Thomas may contain some early and possibly independent traditions, interpreters also see clear signs that Thomas has edited materials taken from the Synoptics.[8]

One basic distinction between the religious imaginations of Thomas and John involves the locus, or "place," of salvation. For John salvation comes through Jesus. According to Thomas, Jesus's sayings do open the path to life, but salvation ultimately resides within the individual. A true understanding of the self, of one's own nature as spirit, eliminates the need for an external savior or for a future salvation. Consider logion 3 of Thomas:

> Jesus said, "If your leaders say to you, 'Look, the kingdom is in the sky,' then the birds of the sky will precede you. If they say to you, 'It is in the sea,' then the fish will precede you. But the kingdom is within you, and it is outside you. When you come to know yourselves, then you will be known, and you will understand that you are children of the living Father. But if you will not know yourselves, then you are in poverty, and it is you who are the poverty.

A certain mocking tone comes through in Thomas's language. How silly to think that salvation is "out there" in heaven! (Greek and Coptic both employ a single word for "heaven" and "sky.") Thomas adopts this same tone for many topics, including all kinds of apocalyptic and eschatological speculation.

> The disciples said to Jesus, "Tell us how our end will come about." Jesus said, "Have you discovered the beginning, then, that you are now seeking the end? For where the beginning is the end will come to be. Blessed is the one who stands at the beginning: that one will know the end and he will not taste death." (Gos. Thom. 18)

And,

> His disciples said, "When will you appear to us and when shall we see you?" Jesus said, "When you strip naked without being ashamed and take your clothes and place them under your feet like little children and stamp on them, then you will see the Son of the Living One, and you will not be afraid." (Gos. Thom. 37)

In Thomas, every question posed by "the disciples" shows their misunderstanding and opens the path for Jesus's correction. In these two passages the disciples are pursuing eschatological knowledge, but Jesus rejects such inquiries.

Thomas often adopts a more subtle approach to eschatological matters, especially when we compare Thomas to the Synoptics. For example, when Jesus says, "I have cast a fire upon the world," we might recall John the Baptist's claim that Jesus would baptize people with fire (Matt 3:11; Luke 3:16). In Thomas, however, Jesus keeps things in the here and now: "and look, I am guarding it until it blazes" (Gos. Thom. 10). Likewise, when Jesus says "This heaven will pass away, and the one above it will pass away," we might expect end-time speculation (Matt 24:34-35; Luke 21:32-33; see Rev 21:1). Instead, Thomas focuses upon those who are living and those who are dead *in the present*. Thomas 63 features a parable very much like that of the rich fool in Luke 12:16-21. A rich man gathers many possessions, and then he dies. Luke's version includes a scolding from God: "Fool, tonight you will die." Thomas provides a far simpler conclusion: "but that very night he died. The one who has ears had better listen!"

Thomas outright rejects all apocalyptic categories. It never mentions Satan, angels, or demons. It shows no interest in Jesus as messiah. It never discusses a final judgment. Nor does it mention Jesus's death and resurrection. When Jesus's disciples seek answers regarding issues like the end or even Jesus's *parousia*, Jesus deflects their questions in a mocking tone. In contrast, John's Gospel affirms all these values: Jesus's messianic identity, the reality of Satan and the angels (if not demons), a final judgment, Jesus's resurrection and a future resurrection, and even Jesus's return. On apocalyptic topics, Thomas and John do not see eye to eye.

Yet John shares with Thomas the conviction that people may experience "life" in the present. In comparison with the Synoptics, John tends to emphasize present salvation over future deliverance. John certainly downplays the notion of a final judgment. John never describes what such things might look like and provides no imagery that would correspond to hell, torment, or eternal punishment. Angels and Satan play relatively little role in John; demons do not appear at all. John and Thomas may not be alike, but they do share an emphasis on present salvation and some distaste for some kinds of apocalyptic speculation.

Conclusion: What about Jesus?

To varying degrees, apocalyptic concepts play prominent roles in all four canonical Gospels, while the Gospel of Thomas thoroughly rejects apocalyptic discourse. Mark sets the storyline for both Matthew and Luke, a narrative framed as a great conflict between Jesus, messiah and God's Son, and the forces of evil. During his ministry, Jesus and his disciples announce the kingdom of God, while his pattern of healings and exorcisms demonstrates Jesus's authority over Satan and the demons. Mark's story begins with John the Baptist and his announcement that the Coming One will baptize people with the Holy Spirit. The narrative ends with Jesus having risen from the dead through God's dramatic action. Within this framework, Jesus's ministry begins with the apocalyptic revelation that accompanies his baptism: there he sees the heavens ripped apart while a heavenly voice proclaims his identity as God's son. When Jesus dies we see another tearing and another confirmation of Jesus's identity: the curtain of the temple tears asunder and the centurion confesses Jesus as God's Son. Mark includes a lengthy speech on Jesus's part concerning last things and the coming of the Son of Man, a speech Matthew and Luke edit but retain. The Synoptic plotline is thoroughly apocalyptic.

Matthew and Luke basically follow Mark's story, supplementing it with material of their own. In some ways Matthew and Luke amplify Mark's apocalyptic tones. In both gospels angels get involved in Jesus's birth, a tradition that is absent from Mark, and Jesus's followers actually encounter his risen presence. Matthew devotes special attention to images of a final judgment. But in other very important ways they muffle Mark's apocalyptic intensity, particularly the sense that Jesus's return is imminent. Luke especially tends to locate the kingdom's presence in the here and now—"God's kingdom is already among you" (Luke 17:21)—a tendency that somewhat resembles John's celebration of eternal life in the present. John affirms most of the apocalyptic concerns we have encountered in the Synoptic Gospels, including messianism, interest in Satan and angels (if not demons), and hope for a future resurrection and a final judgment. But John's insistence that salvation and judgment alike occur in the present, particularly in persons' responses to Jesus, somewhat distances John from apocalyptic speculation. For its part, Thomas directly rejects apocalyptic discourse in all its forms.

The diversity among the four canonical Gospels, Thomas, and Q (as it is commonly reconstructed) leads many students to a further question: What about Jesus? Did Jesus draw heavily upon apocalyptic topics or not?

As they stand, all four canonical Gospels give voice to a variety of apocalyptic topics, including messianic speculation, involvement with Satan, angels, and demons, the return of Jesus as Son of Man to bring about a final judgment, and a final resurrection. Many students would conclude that if the four canonical Gospels distort Jesus in these respects, the historical Jesus is basically lost to us. We have no hope of uncovering a more compelling portrait of Jesus from other sources.

Other factors reinforce this commonsense assessment. One way to imagine Jesus would involve a timeline that begins with John the Baptist and moves through Jesus to Paul. This is not to say that John the Baptist represents the entirety of Jesus's cultural inheritance. We are simply positing a relationship of continuity between Jesus and the one who baptized him. Nor are we suggesting that Paul articulated the only viable interpretation of Jesus's teaching in the decades after Jesus's career. Surely he did not. Nevertheless, an apocalyptic Jesus makes sense within the trajectory that ties John the Baptist to Paul.

Most historians regard Jesus as an apocalyptic prophet. Some, however, regard the Gospel of Thomas and its discovery as a game changer. Thomas, of course, rejects all speculation concerning messianism, angels and demons, Jesus's return and a final judgment, and resurrection. Some might regard Thomas as irrelevant to the question of Jesus himself. After all, Thomas stands as an outlier among the earliest gospels, and Thomas has a clear agenda of its own. Nevertheless, the presence of Thomas sheds distinctive light upon other traditions such as Q and the epistle of James. Q, like Thomas, consists almost entirely of sayings attributed to Jesus. While it certainly includes apocalyptic topics, Q, like Thomas, never mentions Jesus's resurrection (or crucifixion) directly and never refers to Jesus as the messiah. But Q does inquire whether Jesus is the "coming one" (Luke 7:19; Matt 11:3) and frequently refers to him as the Son of Man. Q also envisions a general resurrection and final judgment (11:31-32; Matt 12:42). For those who believe Q began with an original layer that rejects apocalyptic concerns, the Q-Thomas connection becomes important: two independent texts would present a Jesus who is not shaped by apocalyptic discourse.

Enter the epistle of James. Many include James among our earliest Christian documents. This is a minority view, but it must be taken seriously. (Was James actually written by Jesus's brother of that name?) James mentions Jesus's death only once (5:6) and never alludes to his resurrection, and it draws heavily upon Jesus's teachings for its instruction—overlapping quite a bit with Q, but with a tendency to resemble Matthew more than Luke.

Saying in James	Parallel in Canonical Gospels
1:4 "so that you may be fully mature, complete, and lacking in nothing."	Matthew 5:48

1:5 "Anyone who needs wisdom should ask God"	Matthew 7:7; Luke 11:9
1:6 "Ask in faith, without doubting"	Matthew 21:21; Luke 17:6 (a case in which James resembles Matthew more than Luke)
2:5 "Hasn't God chosen those who are poor by worldly standards to be rich in terms of faith? Hasn't God chosen the poor as heirs of the kingdom he has promised to those who love him?"	Matthew 5:3; Luke 6:20 (a case in which James resembles Luke more than Matthew)
2:14 "My brothers and sisters, what good is it if people say they have faith but do nothing to show it?" (see 1:22)	Matthew 7:21; Luke 6:46
2:15 "Imagine a brother or sister who is naked and never has enough food to eat . . ."	Matthew 25:35-36
3:12 "My brothers and sisters, can a fig tree give olives? Can a grapevine produce figs?"	Mathew 7:16
4:10 "Humble yourselves before the Lord, and he will lift you up."	Matthew 23:12; Luke 14:11
5:12 "Never make a solemn pledge—neither by heaven nor earth, nor by anything else."	Matthew 5:34-37

Some would identify even more Jesus sayings in James; this is a fairly conservative list. Most importantly, these sayings reflect Jesus as the teacher of moral and spiritual wisdom: with the likely exception of James 2:5, they do not carry an apocalyptic overtone. For this reason some interpreters draw connections between James, Q (especially a hypothetical non-apocalyptic layer of Q), and Thomas, and then a further connection to a non-apocalyptic Jesus.

It may be going too far to portray James as devoid of apocalypticism. Only twice does James explicitly invoke apocalyptic concepts. It once mentions the devil (4:7; see 2:19) and later appeals to the return of Jesus: "Therefore, brothers and sisters, you must be patient as you wait for the coming of the Lord..." (5:7-9). But other passages may well evoke speculation concerning a final judgment. For example, James warns the rich to "weep and wail" concerning the miseries that are coming to them—observing that their garments are moth-eaten and their gold and silver rusty. "You have laid up treasure for the last days" (Jas 5:1-3 NRSV). At this point James sounds very much like Matthew's apocalyptic Jesus, who tells people to store up treasure not on earth but in heaven, "where moth and rust" can't destroy (Matt 6:19-20; see Luke 12:33-34). Likewise, James 4:11-12 warns believers not to judge one another, as only God finally judges. Again, James seems to echo an apocalyptic element from Matthew's appropriation of Q (Matt 7:1; Luke 6:37). And as already seen, James's conviction that the poor in this world will inherit the kingdom (2:5) sounds very much like Q's apocalyptic pattern of reversal (Matt 5:3; Luke 6:20).

Most scholars do not find in the Thomas-Q-James connection compelling evidence for a non-apocalyptic Jesus. As it stands, Q contains quite a bit of apocalyptic material. And while James often draws upon the wise sayings of Jesus, in the end James contains more apocalyptic material than some acknowledge. That leaves Thomas standing alone with its clear anti-apocalyptic agenda.

These days most scholars, though clearly not all, see Jesus as an apocalyptic figure—perhaps a prophet announcing God's imminent eruption into history, even one who regarded himself as the one person God had anointed (the messiah) to inaugurate this new age. We cannot regard the canonical Gospels as clear windows into the words and deeds of Jesus: each gospel has its own agenda and its own thematic tendencies. Yet Mark's overall storyline makes sense. Jesus was baptized by John the apocalyptic prophet. He proclaimed the nearness of God's reign among mortals. He gathered disciples to combat the supernatural forces of evil. He believed in a resurrection and a final judgment. Acting with divine authority, he forgave sins and invaded the temple. He may have appointed twelve of his disciples to judge the reconstituted Israel. In the end his followers came to believe God had raised him from the dead and to await his return. That narrative arc accounts for the progression from John the Baptist through Jesus to Paul and other early Christian authors. If it is inaccurate, we know very little about Jesus. If it is accurate, we know quite a bit.

For Further Reading

Allison, Dale C., Jr. *The Jesus Tradition in Q.* Harrisburg, PA: Trinity Press International, 1997.

Eve, Eric C. S. "The Synoptic Problem without Q?" Pages 551–70 in P. Foster, A. Gregory, J. S. Kloppenborg, and J. Verheyden, eds. *New Studies in the Synoptic Problem.* BETL 239. Leuven: Peeters, 2001.

Goodacre, Mark. *Thomas and the Gospels: The Case for Thomas's Familiarity with the Synoptics.* Grand Rapids: Eerdmans, 2012.

Kloppenborg, John S. *The Earliest Gospel: An Introduction to the Original Stories and Sayings of Jesus.* Louisville: Westminster John Knox Press, 2008.

———. *The Formation of Q: Trajectories in Early Christian Wisdom Traditions.* Studies in Antiquity and Christianity. Philadelphia: Fortress Press, 1987.

Levison, John R. "Holy Spirit." Pages 2.859–79 in *NIDB*. Nashville: Abingdon Press, 2007.

Parsenios, George L. *Rhetoric and Drama in the Johannine Lawsuit Motif.* WUNT 258. Tübingen: Mohr Siebeck, 2010.

Chapter Six

The Big Show: Revelation

If we bring up apocalyptic literature, almost everyone immediately thinks of the book of Revelation. Indeed, Revelation gives apocalyptic literature its name: in Greek the book's first word is *apokalypsis*. In many churches the book is known not as "Revelation" but as "the Apocalypse." This Greek noun, along with its cognate verb, has to do with revealing or uncovering. It involves bringing out into the open something that has been hidden. In that sense, apocalyptic literature reveals heavenly mysteries to its audiences, information concerning either heaven and/or hell on the one hand, or the end of history on the other. Revelation performs both functions. Its author, John, ascends into the heavenly realms (Rev 4:1), where he also sees the resolution of history in the defeat of evil and the descent of the New Jerusalem.

> **Rapture Theology**
>
> The rapture is a doctrine common in some Christian circles. Rapture theology posits that Jesus will return not once but twice at the end of history. At his first return, Jesus will gather all believers, living or dead, to meet him in the air and move on to heaven. Most rapture believers think this event will precede a seven-year "tribulation," in which earth will descend into chaos. After seven years, Jesus will return again to reign over all things. Adherents of rapture theology often teach that the Bible has predicted the course

> of history and that current events show that Jesus' return will happen very soon.
>
> Oddly, Revelation does not include a rapture. Rapture theology imports the concept into the storyline of Revelation from texts like 1 Thessalonians 4:13-18; Mark 13:26-27; Matthew 24:37-42; and Luke 17:34-35. This approach mixes and matches passages from various parts of the Bible and fits them into a single narrative for end-time expectation.
>
> Rapture theology holds a prominent place in many religious bookstores. Popular expressions of rapture theology include the *Left Behind* series of novels by Tim LaHaye and Jerry Jenkins and a 2015 movie, *The Rapture*.

Not many people have actually taken the time to read Revelation, but that doesn't stop them from believing they know what's inside. Revelation has so permeated our culture that people know it includes angels and beasts, bizarre symbols like the four riders, and cosmic destruction. They might also assume Revelation includes details it does not in fact contain, such as a rapture or the antichrist. Revelation's representation in both art and pop culture creates a flexible fund of images that nourish phenomena that range from the television drama *Sleepy Hollow* to the film comedy *This Is the End*. Setting aside what we *think* we know about Revelation, what is this last and most vexing book in the Bible?

> ### Revelation: A Quick Overview
>
> From a literary point of view, Revelation has basically two parts, each with its own framing material.
>
> In chapters 1–3 John introduces himself to the seven churches, then describes his encounter with the risen Jesus. The vision itself begins at 1:9. In chapters 2–3 Jesus dictates letters to be sent to seven churches.
>
> Revelation 4:1 marks a turn in the story. John is invited to enter heaven, and he reports the rest of the apocalypse from that point of view. All the narrative action happens here: sequences of judgments and conflicts, followed by a final judgment and the descent of a New Jerusalem down from heaven. The book closes with affirmations of its own authority (22:6-21).

"The" Apocalypse

Not only does Revelation identify itself as an apocalypse with its very first word, it actually represents the New Testament's only literary apocalypse. That is, Revelation is the only New Testament book that is an apocalypse in its entirety: the revelation of an otherworldly vision concerning ultimate things, mediated via guidance and commentary from heavenly beings. Revelation comes with the works: opaque signs and symbols, including composite beasts; encounters with good and evil heavenly beings; cosmic chaos and conflict; a resurrection and final judgment; stories concerning the visionary's personal experience of the vision, including moments of incomprehension and failure; a tour of heaven and one of the heavenly city come to earth; and the resolution of all things. The Bible's only other literary apocalypse is Daniel.

Revelation surely qualifies as an apocalypse, but it also appeals to two other types (or genres) of literature: prophecy and letter. These generic hints occur very early in the book (Rev 1:3-4), and they resound in other sections as well. Prophecy has to do with divine communication mediated by mortals for mortals. When Revelation refers to itself as prophecy, it almost always does so in appealing to its own trustworthiness and authority. For example, Revelation blesses those who hear and keep the words of its prophecy (1:3; 22:7), but it curses those who supplement or detract from it (22:18-19). Allusions to Revelation's status as authoritative prophecy occur very close to its beginning and its ending, suggesting a strong emphasis on the point.

Revelation also introduces itself as a letter. It identifies specific authors and a specific audience. The audience consists of seven churches in Roman Asia, in what today we'd call western Turkey. Almost all interpreters take this identification seriously. Early Christianity flourished in that region, and the concerns Revelation addresses fit those contexts. In some sense Revelation seems to be an actual letter addressed to actual people, perhaps with individual copies for each one of the churches.

The author matter is more interesting: first John blesses the seven churches with grace and peace from God, an echo of Paul's standard letter formula. But Revelation adds another author. It is the "apocalypse of Jesus Christ, which God gave to [or by] him" (1:1, literal translation).

Early in the apocalypse John encounters the risen Jesus, who then dictates individual letters to each one of the seven churches. The letters all feature several common components:

- greetings from Jesus himself, most alluding to some aspect of his description from Revelation 1:12-20;

- an assessment of the status of the particular church, including commendations, admonitions, or both;

- a promise of reward or punishment, depending on that church's response to the message, and a reward for "those who emerge victorious"; and

- a call, "If you can hear, listen to what the Spirit is saying to the churches."

According to the letters, some of the churches are performing better than others. Some receive encouragement or consolation, while others receive warning. Some letters feature a mix of these modes of address. Chapters 2–3 offer seven individual letters within the one larger letter. At one level John is Revelation's author, but he attributes his work to God.

The ultimate purpose of an apocalypse involves revealing the truth from a heavenly perspective. As we have seen, the Greek verb *apokalyptō* means to uncover or reveal. Revelation sets forth a vision of the heavenly realm, how God's world interacts with mortals, and what the future entails. Like other apocalypses, however, Revelation also unmasks a deeper truth that underlies common perception: how things "really" are from a divine perspective. Sometimes apocalypses clothe their reality in fairly straightforward terms, like allegories. In Daniel 7, for example, the series of four beasts corresponds to four historical empires that dominated Israel and Judah. On other occasions apocalypses function more allusively, like poetry. Revelation works both ways, challenging interpreters to discern between "decoding" its images and allowing them to remain somewhat vague, general, and elusive.

The Circumstances

Revelation clearly indicates the region in which it emerged and to which it is addressed, the metropolitan centers of Roman Asia. But the book never gives away the time of its composition. Nor does John spell out his motivations for writing—not in a direct or explicit way, in any case. That leaves interpreters reading between the lines for clues.

Sometimes it's helpful, even essential, to identify the date at which a document emerged. And sometimes it isn't. We can enjoy many of Shakespeare's sonnets without knowing by whom or exactly when they were composed. We might imagine the Bard writing about a particular relationship: wouldn't we love to have those details? But we would just as easily enjoy those poems if we learned that someone else had actually composed them. And we appreciate them without knowing the other particulars. All we need is to recognize how sonnets work and to know enough about early modern English. How precisely do we need to grasp Revelation's context in order to read it with a measure of understanding?

Those interpreters who seek to determine Revelation's date tend to fall into two camps. The larger group follows church tradition, as recorded by Irenaeus, who died around 202 CE and claimed that John received his visions in the later years of Domitian's reign. This suggests a date of 95 or 96 CE. Others suggest that Revelation must have been composed before the fall of Jerusalem, likely in 68 or 69 CE. They base this view largely upon Revelation 11, which refers to the "holy city" with its "temple" (11:1-2) and to the "great city...where also their Lord was crucified" (11:8). These interpreters maintain the book must have been written prior to Jerusalem's destruction in 70.

These two main views must also reckon with Revelation 17:9-10, which interprets the beast's seven heads as seven mountains, a fairly clear allusion to Rome as the "city on seven hills." But John provides a double interpretation: "They are *also* seven kings. Five kings have fallen, the one is, and the other hasn't yet come. When that king comes, he must remain for only a short time" (emphasis added).

Without going into too much detail, the two camps agree that the passage provides a counting of Roman emperors. They simply disagree as to which emperor begins the series and which ones to include.

The question of date can affect our interpretation of Revelation in important ways. One issue involves the nature of the crisis, or perceived crisis, to which John is responding. If Revelation was written in the 60s, it could be responding to double calamities: the intense persecution of Christians in Rome by the emperor Nero in 64 CE and the chaos surrounding the First Jewish Revolt of 66–70 CE. If that's the case, Revelation represents a case of anti-imperial resistance literature that stands in solidarity with the larger Jewish (or Judean) communities of the Mediterranean world. Even in Asia, Jewish communities, including those devoted to Jesus, could be seen as standing in solidarity with the revolt. It does seem that Revelation draws upon a somewhat bizarre tradition that emerged in some early Christian circles: the idea that Nero would return from the dead to persecute Christians. (See box below.) The question of date has at least one other dimension: Revelation twice alludes to "Satan's synagogue" (2:9; 3:9). Given the legacy of violent Christian anti-Semitism, these allusions certainly demand attention. An early date, according to which Revelation stands in solidarity with the Jewish people, would suggest that those references function as internal polemic: one Jewish group against others. But the later date suggests that perhaps we have (perhaps Jewish) followers of Jesus who perceive a thorough break from the synagogues in their cities.

Given such mixed evidence of varying degrees of clarity and relevance, many interpreters have given up on assigning Revelation a particular date. Still others, most notably David Aune, have suggested that Revelation is a composite work. According to this view, some parts likely originated in the late 60s, while the book reached its final form in the mid-90s.

I am among those who are skeptical regarding our chances of pinning down Revelation's date. However, I do think we may say some helpful things about Revelation's context. One of the most crucial pieces of evidence involves the letters to the seven churches in chapters 2–3. They may not tell us everything we want to know, but they do offer some hints.

> **The Nero Myth**
>
> Nero reigned as emperor from 54 to 68 CE. The worst calamity that occurred during his reign involved a great fire that destroyed as much as half the city. In an attempt to evade criticism for the fire and its effects, Nero turned the blame on Christians in Rome and subjected them to brutal deaths. The Roman historian Tacitus, who did not remember Nero fondly, recalls some Christians being offered to the wild beasts in the Coliseum, crucified, or burned (*Annals* 15.44).
>
> Although it was only local and short-lived, Nero's persecution burned itself into Christian imagination. Some Christians began to describe Nero returning from the dead to persecute the church, a tradition we find in multiple sources (see especially *Sibylline Oracle* 5.137-154; *Ascension of Isaiah* 4:1-14). In Revelation one of the beast's heads has received a mortal wound that had miraculously healed (13:3, 12; see 17:8, 11), a very likely allusion to Nero's return. Although Revelation may allude to this belief only figuratively, some people apparently did expect Nero's actual return.

First, the letters indicate a movement that has achieved some sense of its own identity. The communities addressed are *churches*, not synagogues. Not only does the movement have shape, the churches in various cities appear to be in communication with one another. Such networking constitutes a distinctive feature of the early Christian movement.

Second, the letters reveal diversity and conflict within and among the churches. For example, John addresses the churches in Ephesus, Smyrna, Pergamum, and Philadelphia as if they are experiencing degrees of conflict with the outside world. The church in Laodicea, by contrast, seems socially and materially comfortable, especially compared with the ones in Smyrna and Philadelphia. Some churches receive commendation for their faithfulness, while others hear a harsher message. Perhaps most striking, several of the letters suggest divisions within the churches. Only "a few" in Sardis are living faithfully, from John's point of view. Meanwhile, the letters condemn prophets who stand in apparent conflict with John: the Nicolaitans (2:6, 15), someone code-named Balaam (2:14), and someone code-named Jezebel (2:20-24). The letters indicate divisions regarding these competing teachers: some follow them, and some reject them. We will investigate these prophets below.

Third, the letters include some traces of persecution. The question of persecution poses one of the most controversial topics in the interpretation of Revelation. Some interpreters believe Revelation was composed in response to intense persecution. That is the traditional view. But an emerging consensus observes that almost all the evidence we have for persecution of Christians comes from the Christians themselves. Apart from hints in these letters, and they are only hints, we have no evidence for persecution of Christians in Roman Asia in the last few decades of the first century CE. Two Greek words factor into this conversation: *hypomonē* and *thlipsis*. *Hypomonē* ordinarily means endurance, but in Revelation is seems to indicate something more like fortitude in trying circumstances. *Thlipsis* can refer to any kind of pressure or difficulty, but Revelation often links it with the hardship that attends persecution. Several of the letters suggest some sort of suffering due to external pressure.

Ephesus	enduring (2:3)
Smyrna	• experiencing tribulation (2:9, 10) • do not fear (2:10) • some about to experience prison (2:10) • be faithful to the point of death (2:10)
Pergamum	"Antipas, my faithful witness, was killed among you" (2:13)
Thyatira	enduring (2:19)
Philadelphia	enduring (3:10)

When one looks closely, one sees that only two of the letters clearly indicate what we might call persecution: the reference to prison and the threat of death in Smyrna, and the reference to Antipas's apparent martyrdom in Pergamum. The three allusions to endurance *might* refer to persecution, or they might not.

The Big Show: Revelation

In the light of the letters, however, other aspects of Revelation jump to the forefront. For example, it seems John identifies himself and the churches alike as victims of persecution. Identifying them as partners in the persecution (*thlipsis*), the kingdom, and the endurance (*hypomonē*) that occur in Jesus, John states that he was on the island of Patmos "because of the word of God and my witness [or testimony] about Jesus" (1:9). Revelation often joins the language of testimony (*martyria*) and witness (*martys*) with that of suffering: indeed, our word "martyr" may derive from Revelation's use of the term. Jesus has died as a faithful witness (1:5). So has Antipas (2:13). So do countless believers (6:9; 11:7; 12:11; 20:4). Revelation portrays a hostile world, inhabited by a dragon (Satan; 12:9), a beast who makes war on the saints (12:17; 13:7), and a prostitute who drinks their blood (17:6). To follow Jesus faithfully is to testify, and to testify means risking one's life.

Persecution plays a fundamental role in Revelation's outlook on the world. Moreover, every significant layer of early Christian literature—all four Gospels, Acts, Paul's letters, and other epistles—share this concern. But apart from Nero's persecution, which was both restricted to Rome and short-lived, we have no contemporary evidence for persecution of Christians anywhere in the Roman world during the first century. Moreover, Revelation *mentions* countless martyrs but *names* only one, Antipas (2:13). As a result some interpreters claim that Revelation is discussing "anticipated" or "perceived" persecution or that it blows up local conflicts into a far grander picture. Some interpreters, then, deny that any serious persecution surrounded John and his churches; others imagine localized but occasionally intense conflict; and still others would set Revelation in a generally hostile context.

The Roman imperial cults pose one critical but contentious point in these debates. Without question Roman Asia exerted enormous energy in honoring both empire and emperor. Cities placed bids before the Roman Senate, competing for the privilege of hosting imperial festivals or building temples to the emperor. Local patrons paid for the buildings, meals, and costumes that made possible such festivals and shrines.[1] This worship of the emperor apparently lies behind the image of the beast in chapter

13, which emphasizes that the beast receives worship (13:4, 8, 12) and that those who do not worship the beast will be killed (13:15). Revelation pronounces doom upon those who receive the mark of the beast and worship it (14:9-11; 19:20), while it links those who do not receive the mark with the faithful martyrs (20:4).

We know that the imperial cults flourished in Asia, but was worship of the emperor compulsory? The closest evidence for that sort of thing comes from Bithynia, a province that bordered Asia in what we'd now call northern Turkey. Working roughly between 110 and 113, the Roman governor Pliny (the Younger) was confronted by anonymous accusations against Christians. He sought advice from the emperor Trajan, which survives in his collected letters.[2] Pliny did not seek out the Christians, yet somehow he knew they could be tried as criminals simply for being identified as such. We note also that the Roman authorities were not *looking* for these criminals; instead, they are being turned in by their own neighbors. Pliny executed those Christians who maintained their faith even under threat. When accused persons denied their Christianity, Pliny required them to invoke the gods, offer small sacrifices and prayers to the emperor's image, and curse Christ. Thus, Pliny's letter does not reveal why Christians were persecuted but it does indicate that emperor worship played some role in the trials. Pliny further reports that sacrificial activity returned to previous levels in response to his policy.

Strictly speaking, Pliny's correspondence proves nothing about the circumstances in which Revelation was composed. Bithynia was adjacent to Asia, but Pliny was writing no less than fifteen years, possibly more, after John wrote Revelation. Some historians regard Pliny's report irrelevant to understanding Revelation. Others believe Pliny provides evidence that refusing to worship the emperor could be deadly. If someone refused to participate in the festivals and the temples, might they be considered traitors, disloyal to the emperor?

Cast of Characters

Revelation, like all apocalypses, tells a story. More properly, Revelation wraps one story within another. The outside story is that of John and his visionary experience. The inner story, which provides the vast majority of the book's content, features a complex cast of characters. Some of those characters are heavenly beings: the One seated on the throne, the Lamb, the elders, the living beings, and the angels—even the martyrs who reside in heaven. Satan and his angels offer resistance to these heavenly forces. Revelation likewise includes ordinary mortals like Antipas, but it tends to divide people into two groups: the Saints and the "Inhabitants of the Earth." A few of Revelation's characters, often depicted only in symbol, figure so prominently that readers may appreciate introductions.

Jesus, the Lamb

Jesus appears in multiple forms in Revelation. His particularly intense manifestation contributes Revelation's first vision: John finds himself overwhelmed by a Jesus who literally shines with divine light, whose voice resounds like "rushing water," and from whose mouth proceeds a double-edged sword (1:12-20). But in its most compelling image Revelation presents Jesus as a Lamb with seven horns and seven eyes, standing although it had been slaughtered (5:6). This image not only recalls Jesus's crucifixion, it also celebrates his resurrection and proclaims that he has authority over all things. For example, the Lamb's realm of authority includes the fate of the cosmos, reflected in its ability to open the seven seals that bind the heavenly scroll (5:9). The Saints follow the Lamb "wherever he goes" (14:4), and the Lamb ultimately vanquishes the forces of evil. In the end, the Saints dwell in a New Jerusalem, adorned as the Lamb's bride (21:9).

In dramatic fashion the Lamb's initial appearance epitomizes Revelation's larger presentation (5:1-13). John has entered the heavenly throne room, but he weeps when it is revealed that no one there is worthy to open the scroll and its seven seals. One of the heavenly elders commands John to stop crying, for the Lion of Judah has conquered and can open the seals. Yet no lion ever appears. Instead John encounters the Lamb, standing with its mortal wounds. The substitution of lamb for lion says everything about Revelation's understanding of power and of Jesus. Jesus does not primarily wield power by violence; instead, Jesus's power comes through his own vulnerability, through his faithful endurance of death. Revelation presents Jesus as a lamb, rejecting a lion Jesus.

The Saints

Revelation presents those who follow Jesus in several ways. They are saints, which literally means holy people. Early Christians did not discriminate between a few special "saints" and the many ordinary believers, as many do today. Instead, the term "saints" includes all believers in Christ. The Saints suffer violence from the Lamb's adversaries, particularly because they do follow the Lamb.

The Inhabitants of the Earth

The Saints constitute a tiny minority of the earth's population so far as Revelation is concerned, the rest of humanity being included among "the Inhabitants of the Earth" (NRSV; CEB, "those who live on earth"). Every allusion to these people is neutral or negative. The Inhabitants face a period of testing (3:10) that turns out to be far more severe. The martyrs who surround the heavenly throne blame the Inhabitants for their deaths and pray for vengeance (6:10). The Inhabitants celebrate and gloat when the two witnesses of Revelation 11 meet their deaths (11:10), and they participate in worshiping the beast (13:8, 12, 14) and cavorting with the prostitute (17:2). Although they are deceived (13:14), the Inhabitants align themselves with the forces of evil and cause suffering for the Saints.

As a result of their corruption, the Inhabitants of the Earth suffer from all the plagues Revelation has to offer. Revelation rarely uses the phrase "the inhabitants of the earth" during these trials, but that's precisely who is involved (8:13). They endure torture so severe that they desire death, which flees from them (9:5-6). Despite all their suffering, the Inhabitants do not repent. They continue in their idolatrous, murderous, and immoral ways (9:20-21). The problem is not that they are ignorant: rather than repent, they curse God precisely because of their punishment (16:9-11). Revelation presents the Inhabitants of the Earth in almost subhuman terms: they prefer evil to good, and they do not—cannot?—conceive of repentance. John's outlook on the rest of society is far from positive.

Balaam, the Nicolaitans, and Jezebel

In addition to enemies beyond the churches, John attacks other Christian preachers as well. We encounter Balaam, the Nicolaitans, and Jezebel in the letters to the churches, particularly the letters to Ephesus, Pergamum, and Thyatira. Almost surely these are the names John assigns to his opponents, not their actual names. The name Balaam recalls the non-Israelite prophet who refuses to curse Israel but is later blamed for leading the Israelites into idolatry and sexual bonding with Moabite women (Num 25:1-9; 31:16). Jezebel recalls the notorious queen who promoted the worship of Baal and murdered the prophets of Yahweh (see 1 Kgs 16–21; 2 Kgs 9). We have no other information on the Nicolaitans, but John accuses them of identical offenses to those of Balaam.

What we have are three Christian leaders (or groups, especially in the case of the Nicolaitans) whose teaching John condemns. To call them "false prophets" is to take John's side in the debate, ignoring that (clearly) some of the Christians in Ephesus, Pergamum, and Thyatira found their teaching compelling. John never names the Nicolaitans' teaching, but he accuses Balaam and Jezebel of encouraging people to eat idol-food and participate in sexual transgression (*porneia*). Because John accuses Balaam and Jezebel of the same things, because John associates Balaam with the Nicolaitans (2:14-15), and because Revelation later characterizes Roman imperial power in terms of *porneia* (esp. 17:1-4), most interpreters believe these competing prophets held roughly the same teaching. The ancient world included countless opportunities to participate in idolatry in little household shrines, daily meals, gatherings of civic and trade organizations, and in city life. Apparently these teachers told Christians it was okay to participate in those activities to some degree or to eat the food associated with them. Their position may have resembled the one we encounter in 1 Corinthians 8:4, in which some claimed the liberty to eat whatever and wherever they wanted, saying that an idol "isn't anything in this world," and "there is no God except for the one God." David A. deSilva summarizes their point this way:

> Why...should Christians—to their own hurt and impoverishment—provoke their neighbors unnecessarily by remaining absent from civic festivals and from dinners in the homes of their associates or the dining halls where their patrons and others would hold symposia?[3]

John condemned this teaching with extreme harshness, believing it constituted an endorsement of idolatry.[4]

> **Food Controversies**
>
> After the role of Gentiles in the emerging churches, the question of food constitutes the second most controversial issue in the New Testament. In Mark 7:19 Jesus pronounces all foods clean, but Matthew's retelling of the same scene (Matt 15:1-20) deletes that declaration. The question dominates discussions of the role of Gentiles in the churches in Acts 10–11 and 15, and in Galatians 2. Paul devotes extended reflections on the question in 1 Corinthians 8, 10, and 11, as well as in Romans 14–15. We encounter the question again in three of Revelation's letters to the churches.
>
> Historians must read between the lines to discern what is at stake in these controversies. One item involves Jewish dietary laws and how those laws play out when non-Jews, or Gentiles, enter the churches. The other concern might involve food contaminated by idolatry, whether that means meals that included aspects of pagan worship, as all public meals did, or meat that arrived in the public market after being sacrificed in temples. This second class of food controversies would have reflected social status: the poor rarely received dinner invitations, nor could they afford meat sold on the open market. More prosperous persons, however, would have depended on public meals for their social and professional networks.

It is possible that John's opponents also promoted sexual license, as John accuses them of promoting *porneia*. Although *porneia* specifically points to prostitution, Jews and Christians used the term to cover a wider range of unspecified sexual sins. However, the Hebrew prophets often deployed sexual sin, particularly adultery and prostitution, as a metaphor for idolatry. We see this most clearly in the prophet Hosea but in other settings as well. John's complaint probably has to do with idolatry rather than sexual misconduct. The main point is that John's stance leaves no room for compromise or toleration. His language toward Jezebel is particularly troubling: some see the bed onto which she is thrown as a metaphor for sickness, but the passage also uses the language of adultery and curses her children (Rev 2:20-24).

Outside of the letters to the churches Revelation never again refers to these teacher-prophets.

The Woman Clothed with the Sun

The Woman Clothed with the Sun (and the moon and twelve stars) appears only briefly, in chapter 12. Immediately we learn that she is in the process of giving birth, and then we see a red Dragon prepared to devour her baby. The Woman twice receives miraculous deliverance from the Dragon. Enraged by her deliverance or by the royal child she bears, the Dragon pursues her other offspring, "who keep God's commandments and hold firmly to the witness of Jesus" (12:17).

The Woman's baby, born to rule all the nations and opposed by the Dragon, almost surely represents Jesus in some sense. Her other children portray those who follow Jesus. But what of the Woman? Her clothing—the sun, moon, and the twelve stars—reminds us of a dream experienced by the biblical patriarch Joseph in Genesis 37. In Joseph's dream the sun and moon represented his father Israel/Jacob and his mother Rachel; the stars stand for Joseph and his brothers. In some unspecific way, the Woman seems to connote the people of God: Israel, from whom the messiah and his followers emerge.

The Dragon, Satan

Satan makes few appearances in Revelation, not appearing until chapter 12. Unlike the Woman he pursues, the Dragon's significance is clear. Revelation identifies the Dragon as Satan (12:9). He leads angels in a failed rebellion against the angels of God (12:7-9), but he empowers the Beast with authority (13:2, 4) and continues his rebellion. Eventually the

Dragon meets defeat, to be cast into a lake of fire with the Beast and the False Prophet (20:1-10).

The figure of the Dragon defines the conflict in Revelation. John's resistance against the Beast and the Prostitute amounts to a conflict that takes place on a cosmic scale. If John and his colleagues follow the Lamb, the rest of humanity is in league with Satan.

The Beast and the Other Beast

As his pursuit of the Woman ends, the Dragon stands on the shore. Immediately a grotesque Beast rises from the sea, with ten horns and seven heads, wearing crowns on each of the horns (Rev 13:1). Combining the features of a leopard, a bear, and a lion, the Beast recalls the four beasts of Daniel 7. (Compare Rev 13:1-2 with Dan 7:3-8.) Daniel's four beasts indicate a succession of four empires, but this single monster subsumes all imperial identity into itself. The Beast receives its authority from the Dragon.

Several features indicate that the Beast has something to do with Roman imperial authority, whether the emperor himself, the imperial cult, or the empire as a whole. Interpreters vary in the degree of specificity they assign to the Beast, but some association with Rome seems clear. It rules over all the peoples of the earth (Rev 13:4, 7). Revelation 17:9 identifies the Beast's seven heads as seven mountains: "everyone" knew Rome as the city on seven hills. Specific details concerning the Beast elude many commentators: what are we to make of the seven heads (kings) and ten horns (potential kings)? Some things seem more clear. The worship the Beast receives relates to the imperial cult, and the Beast persecutes the Saints.

Revelation describes "another beast" rising up from the land (13:11-17). This Other Beast, also called the "False Prophet" (16:13; 19:20), promotes and enforces worship of the first Beast. Because it rises up from the land, commentators identity the Other Beast with the local Asian authorities who promoted the imperial cult and may have encouraged its observance. Some Jewish apocalyptic literature portrays the "sea" as the location from which foreign empires oppress God's people; therefore, a beast rising from the land suggests an indigenous reality. Rising from the sea, the Beast provides the primary symbol against which John resists.

The most remarkable thing concerning the Beast may be the ways in which it invites comparisons with the Lamb. Consider these items.

Lamb	Beast
• seven horns and seven eyes	• ten horns and seven heads
• receives worship	• receives worship
• standing as if having been slain	• one head has received a mortal wound
• marries the Bride	• ridden by the Prostitute and devours her
• conquers the Beast	• conquers the Saints
• in the center of the heavenly throne	• receives the Dragon's throne

Clarity and subtlety rarely blend as effectively as they do here. Although Revelation never comes out and says, "The Beast is a wicked and inferior counterfeit of the Lamb, and one must choose between the two," this system of comparisons implies precisely that. Revelation pits the Lamb and its tiny society over against the empire that dominates the world and evokes its wonder.

The Prostitute

Revelation invokes another image for Roman imperial power, the Prostitute or Whore (Rev 16:19–19:4), also identified as the "Great City." It is difficult to specify just how the Whore relates to the Beast. On the one hand, the Whore rides the Beast, suggesting her dependence upon it. Her identification as the Great City blurs the distinction with the Beast's seven heads that also allude to Rome (17:9). The Beast makes war on the Saints, while the Prostitute drinks their blood (17:6). In other words, the association is very, very close. But on the other hand, the Beast and its horns make war on the Prostitute, strip her naked, and "burn her with fire" (17:16). Those who would date Revelation to the late 60s might see this detail as an allusion to the great fire that occurred under Nero's reign, but the actual fire neither destroyed the city nor put an end to its commerce. Meanwhile, Revelation depicts the Great City's destruction through several means: earthquake (16:18-19), defeat by its allies (17:16), and plagues along with fire (18:8-9).[5]

Revelation glories in the Whore's destruction. Particularly revealing are those who lament the city's fall: kings, merchants, and sailors (18:9-20). The kings lament because their system of diplomacy and commerce, labeled by Revelation the "sexual immorality" and "extravagant ways" they shared with the Prostitute, are no longer available. Merchants weep because Rome's fall leaves them with no consumers for their luxury items. And look at the cargo manifest:

> The merchants of the earth will weep and mourn over her, for no one buys their cargoes anymore—cargoes of gold, silver, jewels, and pearls; fine linen, purple, silk, and scarlet, all those things made of scented wood, ivory, fine wood, bronze, iron, and marble; cinnamon, incense, fragrant ointment, and frankincense; wine, oil, fine flour, and wheat; cattle, sheep, horses, and carriages; and slaves, even human lives. (Rev 18:11-13)

The list progresses from luxury items and delicacies to military pieces like horses and chariots (CEB "carriages"), and it concludes with the greatest victims, those sold in Rome's massive slave trade. With the merchants the shipbuilders and sailors mourn the loss of their wealth. The lament that attends the Prostitute's doom reflects the larger system of Roman military domination and economic exploitation.

The New Jerusalem, the Bride

Just as Revelation contrasts the Beast with the Lamb, it also pits the Prostitute against a positive symbol, the Bride. The Prostitute represents Babylon/Rome, and the Bride personifies the New Jerusalem, a holy city that descends from heaven. Babylon is adorned with gold, jewels, and pearls along with scarlet and purple garments; the Bride wears simple white, but precious metals and jewels sparkle all over the New Jerusalem (Rev 21:11-21). Babylon is marked by her haughty behavior; the Bride conducts herself modestly as Roman brides were expected to do.[6]

If the Lamb embodies faithful witness, the New Jerusalem signifies Revelation's ultimate hope. Readers often overlook that the holy city *comes down* from heaven to earth rather than the other way around. God comes to dwell among mortals (Rev 21:3). The emphasis lies not in the earth's destruction but in its renewal. Revelation has consistently condemned not only the Beast but all the Inhabitants of the Earth; indeed, only those recorded in the Lamb's book of life may enter the city (21:27). Yet some signs in Revelation 21–22 extend hope. The new city identifies "humankind" in general as God's peoples (21:3), the nations and their kings will bring their glory into the city (21:24-25), and the tree of life bears fruit "for the healing of the nations" (22:2).

Revelation's Aims

Revelation presents itself not only as an apocalypse (1:1) but also as prophecy (1:3) and as a letter (1:4) that includes other letters (chaps. 2–3). Both prophecy and letter-writing imply communication that seeks to accomplish some end. (By now, we should recognize that apocalypses are no different in that respect.) The question naturally presents itself: What exactly did John seek to accomplish?

On a narrow level John is calling the Jesus devotees of the seven Asian churches to pure and wholehearted devotion to Jesus. He commands them to abstain from practicing sexual immorality (Greek: *porneia*) and eating idol-food. This biblical language does not concern actual sexual behavior; rather, the prophets described Israelites who participated in idolatry as committing sexual sin. The classic example is the book of Hosea, but examples multiply. What really concerns John is the possibility that believers will somehow implicate themselves in the (from his perspective) idolatrous practices that marked daily life in Roman Asia: meals, festivals, and societies that honored the Empire's various gods. That is why Revelation so often invokes the language of whiteness and purity, particularly keeping one's garments clean (Rev 3:4; see 6:11) and withdrawing from any contact with the polytheistic system (18:4).

John is asking a lot. To abstain from the prayers and offerings that attended every aspect of life would alienate some Christians from their families, some from their social connections, and some from professional and civic opportunities. In other words, people might lose their livelihoods. Moreover, John calls the churches to acknowledge their allegiance to Jesus publicly; that is, to "witness" just as Jesus did and just as John has (1:9; 12:11-12, 17). Revelation even raises the specter that believers may experience imprisonment and martyrdom for confessing Jesus and abstaining from Roman religion (2:10, 13; 6:9-10; 12:11-12; 20:4).

No wonder, then, that other Christian leaders—labeled the Nicolaitans, Balaam, and Jezebel—disagreed with John. They apparently taught that compromise with pagan culture was acceptable, perhaps because it seemed so obviously necessary. Remarkably, their position sounds very much like Paul's teaching that what believers eat doesn't matter so long as people take care not to harm one another with their freedom (1 Cor 8:1-13; 10:14–11:1; Rom 14:1–15:13). Nevertheless, John voices no tolerance for dissent in these matters. One of his tasks involves undermining those other teachers, which is precisely what several of the letters to the churches try to do.

John's aims transcend individual purity. They also include a sustained rejection of Roman imperial power, military oppression, and commercial exploitation. It's hard to say whether John's rejection of idolatry stood ahead of his anti-imperial outlook. We can say, however, that the apocalyptic literature of ancient Judaism, especially Daniel, had prepared John to work at both the individual and the political level. Revelation portrays Rome as idolatrous and blasphemous, primarily on account of the imperial cult. Revelation *also* "reveals" Rome as a monstrous Beast and drunken Prostitute that relies upon military and commercial might to bring the world into submission and exploit its wealth.

John faced significant obstacles in this undertaking. Local elites in Asia celebrated Roman glory: "Who is like the beast, and who can fight against it?" (Rev 13:4). From John's point of view his neighbors—the

Inhabitants of the Earth—have fallen under the Beast's spell. Thus, John must not only unmask the Beast's true nature, he must also inspire hope in his audience. In part that effort comes when John shows the vulnerability of the Beast and the Prostitute: the one actually devours the other (17:16). The largest part involves depicting the Lamb's ultimate victory and the arrival of the New Jerusalem. John's appeal to a blessed future expresses itself in every single one of the letters to the churches in chapters 2–3. More subtle still is John's interpretation of Jesus and his appeal that believers should emulate Jesus. Just when we expect Jesus to appear as a fierce lion (see *4 Ezra* 11:37–12:3), John presents the already slaughtered Lamb (Rev 5:5-7). As the Lamb has conquered through his own testimony, even the sword coming from his mouth, so will believers (Rev 1:2, 9; 6:9-10; 12:11, 17; 19:15, 21; 20:4). They, like the Lamb, are called to be faithful witnesses (1:5; 2:13; 3:14).

Why an Apocalypse?

We cannot know the thought process that led John to compose Revelation. John himself reports the experience of a dramatic vision, in which he received a command to write what he's seen (e.g., 1:11, 19; 21:5). At the same time, John clearly knows the conventions of writing an apocalypse, which is precisely what he does. We can easily imagine John sending a letter in which he uses more ordinary language to express his concerns; instead, he relies heavily upon vision and symbol. That choice renders Revelation more difficult to understand, especially as centuries of history separate readers from John's circumstances and the conventions of apocalyptic discourse. But an apocalypse, like poetry, creates possibilities for powerful communication.

Some readers suppose that Revelation is written in a sort of secret code. According to this theory John wanted to avoid the eyes of Roman authorities, who might understand a more straightforward composition and punish him for his work. But Revelation rarely works like a code, in which each symbol can be translated into one and only one meaning. Apocalypses can and sometimes do use symbols in such straightforward ways; the *Animal Apocalypse* (*1 Enoch* 85–90) uses a series of animals to retell Israel's sacred story, each animal or group of animals standing in for a individuals and groups known from biblical history. One of Revelation's most famous symbols, the number 666, seems to reflect a straightforward code. After all, John invites his readers to figure out the code: "let the one who understands calculate the beast's number, for it's a human being's number. Its number is six hundred sixty-six" (Rev 13:18). Likewise, many interpreters have used the Beast's ten horns as a means of identifying the Roman emperor under whose reign John writes. The heads correspond to seven kings: "five kings have fallen, the one is, and the other hasn't yet come" (17:10). The problem is, interpreters have yet to agree in their calculations.

> **666 and the Number of the Beast**
>
> Revelation's invitation to count the number of the Beast has bedeviled interpreters throughout the centuries. If we're dealing with a code, any ingenious suggestion that "fits" a person or an institution into that number might persuade people. People have identified Ronald Wilson Reagan with the number (six letters in each name); more complicated schemes have identified Barack Obama as the Beast.
>
> The number 666 may simply indicate the Beast's unholy imperfection. If seven and three are the numbers of perfection, then 666 indicates a very, very, very imperfect reality. Another possibility is the Roman emperor Nero: in Hebrew the letters of Nero Caesar add up to a value of 666 or 616, depending on how one spells Nero. Remarkably, some ancient manuscripts of Revelation read 616 rather than 666. Calculated this way, either number fits Nero's name.

In general, however, Revelation more closely resembles poetry than code. Consider, for example, how the book creates comparisons between the Lamb and the Beast or between the Prostitute and the New Jerusalem. Likewise, that dramatic moment in which the book reveals not a Lion but a Lamb works more powerfully through image than it could through code or more direct discourse. As poetry, Revelation is designed to "reveal" the truth behind appearances. The Lamb may seem vulnerable: it stands as if it has been slaughtered, after all. Nevertheless, it wields absolute power by means of its testimony. The Beast looks invincible and glorious, and it is indeed menacing, but arrogance and violence constitute its true nature.

The writing of an apocalypse also enables John to claim absolute authority. Obviously, his opponents, such as Jezebel, would challenge John's authority in real life—just as he does theirs. Apocalyptic discourse enables John's claim that his words derive directly from God. He delivers "a revelation of Jesus Christ," reporting "all that [he] saw" (1:1-2). In chapters 2–3 he delivers to the seven churches individual messages he has received directly from Jesus. Having entered heaven through the open door (4:1), John encounters realities other mortals will never see. Readers may debate whether or not John takes things too far, but he pronounces a blessing upon those who obey his message (1:3) while he curses those who would distort it (22:18-19).

Conclusion

Revelation is the New Testament's only literary apocalypse. The final book in the Christian canon, it closes with a vision of the New Jerusalem that looks back to the Garden of Eden story in Genesis 2. As a river flows through Eden to water the garden (Gen 2:10), a river likewise flows through the New Jerusalem (Rev 22:1); and as the tree of life stands in the middle of the garden (Gen 2:9), in the New Jerusalem the tree of life provides a different kind of fruit every month and its leaves provide healing for the nations (Rev 22:2). From the creation of the heavens and the earth in Genesis to the arrival of a new heaven and a new earth in Revelation, many interpreters regard Revelation as a fitting closing to the Bible.

Revelation also constitutes the classic literary apocalypse. Its very first word, *apokalypsis*, provides the genre's name. As a result, Revelation has perhaps exerted an oversized influence on the study of the literary apocalypses. In the past interpreters tended to judge all apocalypses according to Revelation's topical concerns and literary features. Healthy attention to the noncanonical apocalypses has diminished Revelation as a defining apocalypse among scholars, but its status within the canon guarantees its influence in the church and in culture in general.

For Further Reading

Aune, David. *Revelation*. 3 volumes. WBC 52. Dallas: Word Books, 1997, 1998, 1998.

Carey, Greg. *Elusive Apocalypse: Reading Authority in the Revelation to John*. StABH 15. Macon, GA: Mercer University Press, 1999.

Carter, Warren. *What Does Revelation Reveal? Unlocking the Mystery*. Nashville: Abingdon Press, 2011.

deSilva, David A. *Seeing Things John's Way: The Rhetoric of the Book of Revelation*. Louisville: Westminster John Knox Press, 2009.

Friesen, Steven J. *Imperial Cults and the Apocalypse of John: Reading Revelation in the Ruins*. New York: Oxford University Press, 2001.

Huber, Lynn R. *Like a Bride Adorned: Reading Metaphor in John's Apocalypse*. ESEC. New York: T and T Clark International, 2007.

Koester, Craig R. *Revelation*. AYB 38A. New Haven, CT: Yale University Press, 2014.

Kraybill, J. Nelson. *Apocalypse and Allegiance: Worship, Politics, and Devotion in the Book of Revelation*. Grand Rapids: Brazos Press, 2010.

Rhoads, David, ed. *From Every People and Nation: The Book of Revelation in Intercultural Perspective*. Minneapolis: Fortress Press, 2005.

Chapter Seven
Epilogue

This little book has surveyed how early Christian writers relied upon apocalyptic discourse to shape and express their messages. Throughout our study several consistent themes have emerged.

First, we have encountered the *ubiquity* of apocalyptic discourse in early Christianity. We cannot imagine the ministry of Jesus or the emergence of Christianity apart from the contributions of apocalyptic discourse. Jesus may or may not have been literate: the Gospels report his debates over the Torah, while Luke portrays him reading aloud (4:16-20), but historians debate the question.[1] We have no reason, however, to believe Jesus had read the literary apocalypses like *1 Enoch* or Daniel. Nevertheless, the Gospel reports are replete with religious beliefs and literary forms we find in the literary apocalypses. Jesus talks about the coming Son of Man, a final judgment, and a resurrection of the dead, and he engages in conflict with Satan and the demons. Some historians see Jesus outside of an apocalyptic framework: as a moral and spiritual teacher, a keen social critic, or even a mystical prophet. If Jesus was not interested in those apocalyptic and eschatological concerns, the canonical Gospels have him completely wrong (and Thomas gets him right). That's possible, but it leaves us with little basis for knowing anything about him.

Beyond the Gospels, every significant layer of the New Testament relies on these ideas that emerged in Judaism's apocalyptic literature, along with the confession of Jesus's messianic identity. When Paul reminds the Thessalonians of his gospel, it includes the resurrection and return of Jesus the messiah who delivers believers from coming wrath (1 Thess 1:9-10). Paul clearly believes "the end of time has come" (1 Cor 10:11) in the resurrection of Jesus. Even a text like James, noted for presenting moral and communal teaching without once mentioning Jesus's death or resurrection, features a lengthy passage that mentions the last days, Jesus's return, and a final judgment (Jas 5:1-11). Likewise, apocalyptic discourse plays a minor role in books like Hebrews and 1 Peter, but both works make much of Jesus's return. Hebrews interprets Jesus's resurrection as marking the end of the age, and it anticipates his return as judge (e.g., 9:26-28; 10:26-31), as does 1 Peter (e.g., 1:3-5; 4:5). Both books speculate concerning angels (Heb 1:4-14; 2:5-9; 1 Pet 1:12; 3:22), and both envision the risen Jesus sitting at the right hand of God (Heb 1:3, 13; 8:1; 10:12; 12:2; 1 Pet 3:22). Whether it plays as prominent a role as it does in Paul's letters, or is more generally taken for granted as we find in Hebrews, James, and 1 Peter, apocalyptic discourse contributes to every significant section of the New Testament.

Second, we investigated the *sources* of apocalyptic literature. Apocalyptic literature emerged most directly from Israel's prophetic literature. The prophets claimed to speak directly on God's behalf to the people, sometimes relying on visions and auditions to make their points. The great literary apocalypses likewise claim to relate information that comes directly from the divine realm. Visionaries tour the regions of heaven and hell, converse with God and with angels, and describe what they have seen. If the apocalypses tend to seek hope for divine intervention beyond the present age, whether in heaven or at the end of history, this reflects a movement we see in the so-called proto-apocalyptic sections of the Hebrew prophets.

At the same time, apocalyptic literature cannot be tied down to a single stream of influence. Nor may we explain apocalyptic discourse as simply an inevitable development of the prophetic tradition. The literary apocalypses frequently take on concerns from Israel's wisdom traditions, including the workings of the cosmos and the problem of injustice. There's also the matter of influence from diverse cultures around the Mediterranean world and the Ancient Near East. Apocalyptic literature's tendency to divide persons and spiritual forces into camps of good and evil resonates with ancient Persian religion, as does its tendency to divide history into well-defined ages. Fascination with the underworld provides a major topic in the literature of many ancient societies—and how does one report such things unless an intrepid mortal visits those realms and returns? Like every other cultural phenomenon, apocalyptic discourse draws upon rich and varied sources.

Third, throughout this book we have observed the *rhetorical flexibility* of apocalyptic literature; that is, ancient Jews and Christians deployed apocalyptic discourse to accomplish diverse literary and rhetorical goals. Many people readily imagine how apocalyptic literature could be used to scare people into converting or setting their lives straight—the sort of thing we associate with revival meetings, religious billboards, and street-corner preachers. Yet we also have seen Paul weaving apocalyptic argumentation into creative theological responses to the crises that affected his churches, as he does in 1 Thessalonians 4:13-18. In 1 Corinthians we saw how apocalyptic logic fueled Paul's attempts to correct beliefs, attitudes, and behaviors in a difficult situation. We observed the utility of apocalyptic discourse in establishing a speaker's authority on the basis of visionary experience. Not only does Paul buttress his own authority by claiming apocalyptic visions (Gal 1:10-12; 2 Cor 12:1-10), the Gospel stories of Jesus's baptism and temptation do so as well, as does Luke's report that Jesus has seen Satan fall from the sky like lightning (Luke 10:17-20).

Fourth, parts of our study have called attention to a link between apocalyptic literature and *politics*. Judaism's first great political apocalypses, *1 Enoch* and Daniel, express hope for the destruction of prevailing empires and the inauguration of a new kingdom instituted by God. At the same time, *1 Enoch's* oldest sections, the *Book of the Watchers* and the *Astronomical Book*, appear more interested in cosmic mysteries than in political conflict. Some interpreters perceive an implicit political message in the story of the Watchers, who introduce violence and corruption into the world. The Antiochene Crisis, however, and the ensuing Maccabean Revolt gave rise to the kind of apocalyptic resistance literature we encounter in Daniel and the *Animal Apocalypse*. The Qumran *War Rule* and *Habakkuk Pesher* imagine the destruction of the *Kittim*, allusions to the Seleucids or to the Romans, depending upon our assessment of each scroll's date. The New Testament's classic apocalypse, the book of Revelation, follows their model by describing a beastly current empire being displaced by the rule of the Lamb. Later Jewish apocalypses like *4 Ezra* and *2 Baruch* take up this political critique in the wake of the failed revolt of 66–70 CE.

It is less clear, however, how much political significance attaches to the apocalyptic language we encounter in literature such as Paul's letters and the Gospels. Some interpreters regard Paul and the Gospels as self-consciously counter-imperial, while others perceive a more implicit tension between the Jesus movement and Rome. Paul clearly expresses reservations about the age in which he lives, reservations that may reflect disdain for the Roman authorities, "the present-day rulers" who are passing away and who "crucified the Lord of glory" (1 Cor 2:6-8; see Rom 8:38). Disputed Pauline letters like Colossians and Ephesians amplify this language (see Eph 3:10; 6:12; Col 1:16). Some interpreters regard these letters as talking about spiritual rather than sociopolitical forces; however, a reference to Christ's having "disarmed the rulers and authorities" and "exposed them to public disgrace" (Col 2:15) seems to interpret the crucifixion as an exposé of perverted political might. Paul regards the society in which he lives as inherently violent and corrupt. When he proclaims peace and reconciliation in Christ, as he does at the beginning of every letter and dozens of times throughout, that peace runs counter to the peace (*pax Romana*) Rome promises those who submit to it.[2] It is less clear, however, that he targets Rome or the emperor for direct criticism.

The link between political resistance and apocalyptic literature proves just as challenging with respect to the Gospels, especially the Synoptics. When Jesus blesses the poor and pronounces woe to the rich (Luke 6:20, 24; see Matt 5:3), he may refer to a reversal of social status that lies in the future. We might well interpret Luke's parable of the Rich Man and Lazarus among similar lines: a rich man dies and goes to torment, while the poor man he neglected rests in Abraham's bosom (Luke 16:19-31). Jesus's concern for the poor may transcend the judgment of individuals. Similar concern for the poor animates the *Parables of Enoch*, the *Epistle of Enoch*, and the early Christian *Shepherd of Hermas* (e.g., *1 Enoch* 94:6-9; *Hermas* 17:3-5). The link to *Enoch's Parables* is particularly relevant because Jesus's use of the term "Son of Man" resonates strongly with that section of *1 Enoch*, in which the Son of Man/messiah displaces the rulers of the day who oppress the poor. Jesus's self-identification as Son of Man envisions the end of those powers.

Jesus's proclamation of the kingdom, or empire, of God implies an alternative to the empires of his own era. Rome supposedly established an eternal kingdom, but Jesus announces an eschatological kingdom of his own. The Gospels have a way of blurring terms like *kingdom, messiah*, and *Son of Man*—all of which carry political connotations. When asked if he regards himself as Israel's messiah, Jesus turns to Son of Man language—another link with the political dimension of apocalyptic discourse.

> High Priest: "Are you the Christ [messiah], the Son of the blessed one?"
>
> Jesus: "I am. And you will see the Human One [Son of Man] sitting on the right side of the Almighty and coming on the heavenly clouds." (Mark 14:61-62, quoting Dan 7:13; see Ps 110:1)

This pattern, in which Jesus answers a question about the messiah with Son of Man language, appears in all three Synoptic Gospels (see Matt 26:63-64; Luke 22:67-69). It does not occur in John's trial narrative, but John devotes extensive attention to Jesus's identity as "King of the Jews" (John 18:33–19:22). Indeed, the trial narratives in all four Gospels eventually focus on Jesus's identity as King of the Jews (Mark 15:2, 9, 12, 17-18, 26; Matt 27:11, 29, 37, 42; Luke 23:2-3, 37-38). If Jesus is a messianic king, his reign conflicts with that of Caesar but does not resemble Roman rule. Thus, apocalyptic discourse contributes to the Gospels' indirect, perhaps ambiguous, political commentary.

We often encounter apocalyptic discourse beyond what we might call "apocalyptic literature." Revelation provides the New Testament's only true apocalypse. We might label the little apocalypses of Mark 13, Matthew 24, and Luke 21 as apocalyptic literature. But apocalyptic concepts, assumptions, and literary devices occur all over the New Testament, and they function in remarkably flexible ways. Given the diverse literary and cultural streams that contributed to the rise of apocalyptic literature, its widespread influence and application require a multidimensional explanation. On the one hand, we have the tradition of great literary apocalypses. Revelation stands among *1 Enoch*, Daniel, *4 Ezra*, and *2 Baruch*, among other examples of the genre. We also encounter apocalyptic discourse in less formal contexts, beyond the boundaries of the literary apocalypses. Paul adapts it to his letters. Apparently Jesus both was influenced by apocalyptic ideas and incorporated them into his teaching: so far as we know, Jesus did not write. Apocalyptic discourse cannot be limited to a single literary tradition or social movement. Like other cultural phenomena, it surged beyond its boundaries, blending into the fluid dynamics of ancient culture.

Beyond the New Testament

Apocalyptic discourse continues to exert its influence beyond the New Testament documents, most notably in more literary apocalypses. From a historical point of view the New Testament does not represent a "period" of early Christian literature. For example, in his Corinthian correspondence Paul alludes to letters we do not possess (1 Cor 5:9; 2 Cor 7:8), while 2 Thessalonians mentions people who are already forging letters in Paul's name (2:2, 15; 3:17).

Early Christianity produced several literary apocalypses. The *Shepherd of Hermas* held occasional canonical status, included within manuscripts of the Bible and used in the public reading of scripture in some churches. Several important early Christian writers cite *Hermas* as scripture. Quite long, *Hermas* includes a series of five visions, ten mandates devoted to faithful living, and ten allegorical parables that also present instruction in righteousness. Among other concerns, *Hermas* envisions a time of persecution, promoting repentance and warning believers to stand firm under pressure. In the fourth vision Hermas encounters a fearsome beast. Hermas recalls the instruction not to be double-minded and confronts the charging beast, which lies on the ground and puts out its tongue while Hermas passes by (*Hermas* 22:5-10). *Hermas* also has much to say concerning judgment and the afterlife. After baptism, believers are permitted to lapse into sin and repent only one time. Beyond that no hope remains (*Hermas* 6:4-8; 31:1-7; contradicting Heb 6:4-6; 10:29).

> **Reading the Early Christian Apocalypses**
> Translations of *Hermas*, the *Apocalypse of Peter*, and the *Ascension of Isaiah* are available in print but cannot be found within one volume. Free but dated translations of all three works are available online. Mitchell G. Reddish's *Apocalyptic Literature: A Reader* (Peabody, MA: Hendrickson, 2015) includes parts of all three works. Bart D. Ehrman's *The New Testament and Other Early Christian Writings: A Reader* (New York: Oxford University Press, 1998) includes selections from *Hermas* and all of the *Apocalypse of Peter* but none of the *Ascension of Isaiah*.

The *Apocalypse of Peter* imagines the fate of the dead—with particular interest in the suffering of the wicked. The apocalypse begins with Jesus's apocalyptic discourse in Matthew 24. Jesus offers the comparison of the fig tree: just as we recognize the time for fruit, so should disciples recognize that the end is near (Matt 24:32-33). When Peter requests an explanation, Jesus shows the fate of all persons in his right hand. Peter then tours hell, where punishments fit the sinners' characteristic crimes: blasphemers hang by their tongues, adulterous women hang by their hair, and adulterous men hang by their genitals. The apocalypse gives some attention to the fate of the righteous, but it does not detail their rewards as it does the punishments of the wicked. The *Apocalypse of Peter* apparently provides the model for a fourth-century *Apocalypse of Paul*, which in turn influenced Dante's presentation of hell.

The *Ascension of Isaiah* provides a fascinating example of apocalyptic literature's diversity and adaptability. The heart of the story is a Jewish tradition concerning Isaiah's martyrdom: King Manasseh, a notorious biblical villain, has the prophet sawn in two for preaching against the king. Hebrews 11:37 alludes to this legend. In the early second century one or more Christian authors added visions to the narrative, changing its meaning. Among other things Isaiah travels through the seven heavens and observes Jesus, "the Beloved," as he descends to earth. Born of the Virgin Mary, Jesus performs wonders, is crucified and raised, and sends out his apostles with his message. According to these Christian adaptations, Manasseh orders Isaiah's execution on account of his vision of Jesus. Isaiah's ascent to the seventh heaven offers an interpretation of Jesus's incarnation: the Beloved diminishes in glory as he descends from one heaven to the next. The revised story also presents a reinterpretation of the biblical Isaiah: Isaiah "saw" Jesus and predicted him. In their conflicts with Jews, real or imagined, early Christians often turned to Isaiah as a witness to Jesus.

> **Christian Gnosis**
>
> Orthodox Christian authors often vilified a group they called the Gnostics, a term that derives from the Greek word for knowledge. The Gnostics supposedly taught that the material world had been created by an inferior deity and that people could attain salvation through esoteric knowledge. The 1945 discovery of thirteen codices (books with covers) at Nag Hammadi included fifty-two or fifty-three literary works that scholars immediately identified as Gnostic. Today many scholars have grown suspicious that "Gnosticism" ever existed as a unified movement. When we speak of "Gnosis-oriented Christianity," we mean forms of Jesus devotion that promote some kind of mystical knowledge as a means of salvation.

Along with Revelation, *Hermas*, the *Apocalypse of Peter*, and the *Ascension of Isaiah* all seem to have appeared prior to 150 CE or so. Revelation, *Hermas*, and the *Apocalypse of Peter* all attained wide popularity. As time passed, appeals to direct revelation grew controversial among early Christians—and that's putting it mildly. In the middle of the second century a group of prophets named Montanus, Priscilla, and Maximilla claimed inspiration from the Holy Spirit and proclaimed their direct revelations. Their movement continued long after their deaths. Meanwhile, Gnosis-oriented Christianity often relayed its mysteries through its own apocalypses. According to Dylan M. Burns, if one counts revelatory discourses attributed to the post-resurrection Jesus, copies of twenty-six Gnostic apocalypses survive.[3] As conflicting forms of Christianity squared off against one another, the leaders of what would become orthodox

Christianity dismissed the value of independent revelations.[4] A similar process occurred in Judaism.

Millennial Speculation

Many Americans today regard Revelation as a set of predictions regarding the end of history. Polling research consistently demonstrates widespread belief that we are living in the end times, as "predicted" by Revelation. In a 2014 survey the Public Religion Research Institute asked people whether the severity of recent natural disasters is due to climate change or to "what the Bible calls the 'end times.'" While 62 percent of Americans linked natural disasters to climate change, 49 percent said such events demonstrate that we're living in the end times.[5] In 2013 the Southern Baptist LifeWay Research found that nearly one-third of Americans saw US military strikes in Syria having been predicted in Revelation, while one in five believed the world would end in their lifetimes.

Millennialism describes imminent expectation of the last days. The most influential form of millennialism in the United States, dispensational premillennialism, teaches a series of events. First Jesus returns to gather his believers, living and dead alike, in the air and take them to heaven. This event is called the rapture. Seven years of violence and suffering follow the rapture, and then Jesus returns again to bring about the millennium, a utopian period of one thousand years. After the millennium comes the final separation of the righteous from the wicked. Dispensational premillennialism requires complicated cutting and pasting of passages from all over the Bible to form a consistent scenario, a sort of "jigsaw puzzle" approach to the Bible. This teaching is extremely popular in some Christian circles and is particularly evident in religious broadcasting and in bookstores. The twentieth century's most famous evangelist, Billy Graham, promoted an optimistic brand of millennialism, devoting two books to the topic. Graham, it seems, moved from preaching the nearness of the end to encouraging repentance: perhaps God would delay the inevitable end.[6]

Millennial speculation has an ancient pedigree. As the Roman Empire first legitimized and then affirmed Christianity, the church began to discourage millennial speculation. Rather than understanding Revelation as calling for resistance to Roman domination, interpretations saw the book as portraying the history of the church or the progress of the soul. From time to time, however, influential interpreters promoted Revelation as a road map for the end times. The sixteenth-century reformers Martin Luther and John Calvin tended to deemphasize Revelation, to some degree in response to millennial movements such as the Peasants' Revolt of 1524–25 that erupted in horrific violence. Millennial aspirations in part motivated the Puritans who settled Massachusetts, leading them to envision their settlement as a new Israel. The great Puritan preacher Jonathan Edwards kept a notebook in which he speculated concerning the arrival of the millennium.[7]

Low-level millennial expectation is always simmering in American culture, surfacing especially in times of crisis. Cold War anxiety regarding nuclear annihilation boosted sales of Hal Lindsey's bestseller *The Late Great Planet Earth* (1970), while conflict in the Middle East has fueled waves of millennial speculation from one decade to another. Every once in a while, however, millennial hopes have generated spectacular outcomes. In chapter 1 we introduced William Miller, who calculated the date of Jesus's return to between March 21, 1843, and March 21, 1844. When the latter date passed, Miller revised his calculations to April 18, which also passed. Finally, and under pressure from his followers, Miller identified October 22. By the thousands Millerites, as they were known, experienced disappointment, ridicule, and occasional violence from resentful neighbors. The Millerites represent the best-known expression of "mainstream" American millennialism, but more obscure movements like the Branch Davidians have also attained notoriety. Their leader David Koresh gathered the group in a ranch compound outside Waco, Texas. Anticipating that in the last days the United States government would seek to destroy the faithful remnant, they gathered weapons and other supplies. A raid led by the Bureau of Alcohol, Tobacco, and Firearms led to a shootout in which four agents and six Davidians were killed. After a fifty-one–day siege the ATF attempted to storm the Davidian compound, and a fire broke out in which seventy-six people died. The Davidians themselves ignited the fatal fire.[8]

Millennialism's popularity has waxed and waned from context to context, but its basic sentiments—that the Bible predicts the final events and that Jesus will return soon—never disappear. All millennial predictions fail with the passing of time. Perhaps more importantly, would-be prognosticators tend to identify the crises of their own times as signs of the end. In a sense, we encounter the same phenomena in the apocalyptic literature of ancient Judaism and early Christianity. Just as Daniel and parts of *1 Enoch* link the Maccabean Revolt with history's resolution, so does Revelation identify Rome as the ultimate beast. The Synoptic Jesus alerts his disciples to expect "all these things" in this generation (Matt 23:36; 24:34; Mark 13:30; Luke 21:32). Apocalypticism does not always involve end-time speculation, but it often does.

Frameworks for Interpretation

This book's primary goals have involved introducing readers to the diversity and importance of early Christian apocalyptic literature and helping readers to understand that literature in its ancient historical and literary contexts. Nevertheless, many people assume apocalyptic literature is about predicting the end times. If apocalyptic literature does not provide that kind of predictive force, what frameworks might help us understand these texts and interpret them in public contexts? Many readers have found the following frameworks helpful.

First, we may approach apocalyptic literature as *rhetoric*. Rhetoric involves the process by which people attempt to persuade one another, to shape beliefs, attitudes, and behaviors. Early Christians adapted apocalyptic literature to a variety of rhetorical purposes. Revelation encourages believers to resist idolatry and Roman imperialism and its religious trappings. Paul comforts the Thessalonians, corrects the Corinthians, and buttresses his own authority. Matthew and Luke adapt Mark's apocalyptic teaching to their own circumstances and thematic interests. In Revelation's seven letters the churches receive custom blends of praise, comfort, scolding, and encouragement. Reading apocalyptic literature rhetorically raises questions like, *What is this text asking of its audience? What is the author trying to accomplish in this text? How might early Christian audiences have responded to this literature?*

Second, many instances of apocalyptic literature resemble *poetry*; that is, they express themselves through the evocative language of metaphor and symbol. Jesus is not a literal lamb, nor is the Roman Empire a monster, but in Revelation a network of poetic comparisons establishes the sharp distinction between what it means to worship the Lamb and what it means to serve the Beast. Likewise, the depiction of Jesus in Revelation 1:12-20 makes no literal sense, but it contributes heavily to the rest of the book. To take one example, the risen Jesus walks among seven lampstands, which are interpreted as the seven churches addressed by the book. One could say that Jesus is mystically present among these vulnerable Christian communities; even that sentiment defies straightforward expression. Much more evocative, however, is the image Revelation provides.

Poetry always involves a measure of excess. No set rules provide the key for interpreting every symbol, image, or metaphor we encounter. Nor do we always know how to distinguish metaphorical and symbolic language from literal language. For example, several early Christian texts describe the Son of Man coming in the sky (Mark 14:62; Matt 24:30; 26:64; Rev 1:7). Paul describes believers rising up in the clouds to meet Jesus at his return (1 Thess 4:16-17). This imagery derives from Daniel 7:13, which adapts even more ancient depictions of God as riding upon the clouds (e.g., Pss 68:4; 104:3). We cannot know whether Paul, for example, literally believes that believers will meet Jesus in the clouds or instead deploys conventional imagery to describe an event that transcends language. In either case, we have good reason to assess the poetic dimension of images like the darkening of the sun (e.g., Mark 13:24; Matt 24:29; Luke 21:25; Acts 2:20; Rev 6:12; 9:2) and riding on clouds. These images attained a conventional status in apocalyptic literature, connoting a fundamental break from the ordinary processes of human life.

Third, apocalyptic literature often amounts to a form of *constructive theology*. Constructive theology does not involve inventing theological ideas out of thin air; instead, it draws upon traditional sources of wisdom in addressing new problems and cultural moments. Apocalyptic texts often develop creative resolutions to emergent problems. Daniel, for example, provides our first documented witness to belief in a resurrection of the dead and sorting of the righteous from the wicked (Dan 12:1-3). But Paul faces a different problem: he's promised Jesus's return, but how does he address believers in Corinth who seem to regard the resurrection concept as silly? Paul first works through why Jesus's resurrection implies a more general resurrection in the future (1 Cor 15:12-28). Second, he tries to explain why the idea of a risen body isn't ridiculous: "When you put a seed into the ground, it doesn't come back to life unless it dies" (15:36), and plants scarcely resemble the seeds from which they have sprung (15:37-38). Likewise, when Revelation promises to introduce a Lion but presents a Lamb instead, we have a creative interpretation of power. In Revelation the Lamb conquers not with military force as Rome does (Rev 13:4) but with the word of its faithful testimony. So will the Lamb's followers (Rev 1:5; 12:11; 19:15, 21). Apocalyptic discourse need not rely upon ordinary discursive language to perform constructive theology; it does so largely through metaphors, symbols, and word images.

Relevance

We have established that apocalyptic discourse contributed to the emergence of Christianity in fundamental ways. It supplied ideas like messianic expectation, a final judgment, and the resurrection of the dead that proved essential to Christian imagination, along with perhaps less central concepts such as Satan and the demonic realm. Apocalyptic discourse shows up at every level of the New Testament. Therefore, an understanding of apocalyptic literature is necessary for understanding the early Christian movement.

We might also imagine whether and how apocalyptic literature might prove relevant for contemporary readers. Many do not share belief in angels and demons. Whatever happens after we die, and whatever we may hope to be the case, resurrection language may not persuade all modern people. When a contemporary person claims to have experienced a revelation directly from God, we tend toward suspicion rather than credulity.

Epilogue

If our fundamental convictions do not conform to apocalyptic categories, does this literature bear any significance?

I would respond to the question of relevance at two levels, one specifically theological and one of more general interest. Those who read the Bible theologically will find meaning in it even when they do not share the assumptions of its authors. For example, few of us believe God created the world in seven literal days just over six thousand years ago. Modern genetics has ruled out the possibility that humankind can be traced to just two human ancestors. We don't believe in a seven-day creation or a literal couple named Adam and Eve, but we still find Genesis's creation stories theologically relevant. They communicate God's beneficent intentions for creating the world. They celebrate human relationality. They grapple with the problems of suffering, maturation, disobedience, and mortality. The biblical authors may have thought heaven was some place "above" the earth, an assumption reflected in Genesis, yet readers still find the book compelling.

As for apocalyptic literature, we might take resurrection as a case study. Here I will speak confessionally. I cannot get my mind around resurrection as a literal concept. Paul writes that our bodies will be mystically transformed (1 Cor 15:42-54). Revelation sings that death and Hades will return the bodies of the dead—even the sea will give back its dead (Rev 20:13)! I cannot make literal sense of either idea.

Yet I value the concept of a resurrection extremely highly. Early Christians wrangled over the relative value of the body. Some believed that bodies were more of a hindrance than a blessing: yes, they bring pleasure, but they will necessarily experience pain, decay, and other limitations. What mattered, these people said, was the spirit. Others, however, insisted that bodies mattered. It mattered that Jesus was truly and fully human. And it mattered that God raises our bodies. For these believers an "immortal soul" was not sufficient. Thus, the Apostles' Creed confesses not the immortality of the soul but "the resurrection of the body."

Apocalyptic literature confronts us with the question of resurrection, and I am grateful for the concept. I do believe bodies matter, and I am committed to a Christian faith that values our bodies and how our bodies relate to those of others and to the world around us. I would not pretend to understand, or even to believe, the literal concept of a resurrection. Yet it is through study of apocalyptic literature that I have come to appreciate the significance of this question. Whatever lies beyond death, I hope God reclaims and redeems our entire embodied lives.

Apocalyptic literature also draws a connection between ultimate hope and daily life concerns. It suggests that a transcendent reality lies behind the things that concern us from day to day. Most of the time we do just fine pursuing an education, enjoying relationships, making meaningful contributions, making time for play and pleasure. But other moments confront us. Sometimes we experience personal loss that threatens our ability to live with joy and freedom. Alternatively, we also face challenges at the social, cultural, and global levels that frustrate our ability to provide solutions. These problems can seem intractable. Apocalyptic literature insists that a greater reality stands behind our struggles for justice and wholeness. Martin Luther King Jr. was fond of saying, "The arc of the moral universe is long, but it bends toward justice." Apocalyptic literature claims to "unveil" or "reveal" an ultimate truth that lies beyond our challenges, and it promises a divine resolution that may not fit our expectations or hopes.

One remarkable quality of apocalyptic literature is that while it seems otherworldly, it often inspires daily action on a very practical basis. Revelation calls its audience to resist not only the worship of Rome and its emperor but also the commercial and military systems of that empire. The *Shepherd of Hermas* admonishes wealthy believers to look out for the poor, a value shared in the epistle of James's most heavily apocalyptic passage (Jas 5:1-6). As we have seen, Paul directs the heady teaching concerning the resurrection in 1 Corinthians 15 not toward abstract speculation but toward just relationships within the community. Apocalyptic literature articulates the connection between our overarching values and our daily behavior.

In many respects apocalyptic literature resembles science fiction. Both genres imagine an alternative reality, in which they invite their audiences to walk around. (We could say similar things about other genres like fantasy literature.) Science fiction tends to take very here-and-now problems and project them into a futuristic setting. *Star Trek* emerged during the social and racial strife of the 1960s, and it frequently depicts encounters across cultures—not to mention a racially and ethnically diverse cast. (The series also receives complaints regarding its depiction of race.) In the Cold War era *Star Wars* pitted democracy against militaristic totalitarianism, a theme that has been downplayed in the series' later incarnations. Other science fiction examples explore problems like climate change and environmental degradation, gender difference and discrimination, human dependency upon technology, and devastating viruses. Science fiction, like apocalyptic literature, addresses contemporary anxieties by imagining alternative worlds. The primary difference lies in the value attached to that other world. In science fiction the alternative setting primarily provides a location for the working out of conflict; in apocalyptic literature the alternative world embodies the fundamental values to which readers should devote themselves.

For Further Reading

Boyer, Paul. *When Time Shall Be No More: Prophecy Belief in Modern American Culture.* Cambridge, MA: Belknap Press, 1992.

Burns, Dylan M. "Apocalypses among Gnostics and Manicheans." Pages 358–72 in *The Oxford Handbook of Apocalyptic Literature.* Edited by John J. Collins. New York: Oxford University Press, 2014.

Frykholm, Amy Johnson. "Apocalypticism in Contemporary Christianity." Pages 441–56 in *The Oxford Handbook of Apocalyptic Literature.* Edited by John J. Collins. New York: Oxford University Press, 2014.

Gorman, Michael J. *Becoming the Gospel: Paul, Participation, and Mission.* Grand Rapids: Eerdmans, 2015.

Jones, Robert P., Daniel Cox, and Juhem Navarro-Riverra. "Believers, Sympathizers, & Skeptics: Why Americans Are Conflicted about Climate Change, Environmental Policy, and Science: Findings from the PRRI/AAR Religion, Values, and Climate Change Survey." Washington, DC: Public Religion Research Institute, 2014.

Keith, Chris. *Jesus Against the Scribal Elite: The Origins of the Conflict.* Grand Rapids: Baker Academic, 2014.

Koester, Nancy. "The Future in Our Past: Post-millennialism in American Protestantism." *Word & World* 15 (1995): 137–44.

Newport, Kenneth G. C. *The Branch Davidians of Waco: The History and Beliefs of an Apocalyptic Sect.* New York: Oxford University Press, 2006.

Pagels, Elaine. *Revelations: Visions, Prophecy, and Politics in the Book of Revelation.* New York: Penguin Books, 2012.

Smolenski, Reiner. "Apocalypticism in Colonial America." Pages 36–71 in *The Encyclopedia of Apocalypticism: Volume 3: Apocalypticism in the Modern Period and the Contemporary Age.* Edited by Stephen J. Stein. New York: Continuum, 2000.

Swartley, Willard M. *Covenant of Peace: The Missing Peace in New Testament Theology and Ethics.* Grand Rapids: Eerdmans, 2006.

Wessinger, Catherine. "Apocalypse and Violence." Pages 422–40 in *The Oxford Handbook of Apocalyptic Literature.* Edited by John J. Collins. New York: Oxford University Press, 2014.

Notes

Chapter One—A Thought Experiment

1. Arrested Development, "Fishin' 4 Religion," from *3 Years, 5 Months & 2 Days in the Life Of...* (1992).

2. N. T. Wright 310–12.

3. Collins and Collins 75–100; Wright 307–20.

4. Josephus, *Antiquities* 18.1.4; *War* 2.8.14.

5. Richter 2012; deSilva 2012: 126, 139.

6. For an introduction to the major ancient Jewish and Christian apocalypses, see Carey 2005.

7. Keith.

8. Stephen Stein, 1998: 114.

9. O'Leary 108.

10. Bauckham 1998; Clark-Soles 2006; Segal 2004.

Chapter Two—Apocalyptic Literature in Context

1. Collins 1998; Carey 2005. Other textbooks offer more comprehensive introductions to ancient Jewish apocalyptic literature.

2. Collins 1998: 32–33; Collins, *Daniel* 11.

3. Bremmer 2014: 343–44; see Himmelfarb 1983: 58.

4. See Newsom 2014: 302.

5. Cook 1995; Sweeney 2005: 239–40.

6. Cook 2014: 28–29.

7. Levenson 2006; Segal 2004.

8. Collins, *Jewish Wisdom*, 184.

9. Wright and Wills 2005; Goff 2014: 61–63.

10. Grabbe 2003: 118–19.

11. deSilva 2012: 101–40.

12. Portier-Young 2011.

13. Goff 2011: 230.

14. Newsom 2014: 12–21.

15. Portier-Young 2011: 219.

16. Portier-Young 227.

17. VanderKam 2010.

18. Beyerle 2014: 381.

19. Carey 2005: 160–61.

Chapter Three—The Pauline Epistles

1. Taylor 2012: 35–39; Roetzel 1997: 178–83.

2. Boyarin 1994: 1–3.

3. Segal 1990: xi.

4. Roetzel 1999: 38–42.

5. Allison 1998: 122–29.

6. Kloppenborg 1987.

7. Allison 1997.

8. N. T. Wright 1992: 328–31.

9. Josephus, *Antiquities* 18.1.3; *War* 2.8.14.

10. Charlesworth 2009: 4.377–78.

11. Segal 2004: 377–78, 493.

12. Carey 1999: 56–57, 77–92.

13. See de Boer 1998: 346–47.

14. See Gaventa 2013.

15. Bassler 2007: 35–47.

16. Bassler 2007.

17. Dunn 1998: 102–27.

18. See the classic essay on this topic by Wayne A. Meeks (1983).

19. Aristotle, *Rhetoric* 1.2.1.

20. Bauckham 1998; Clark-Soles 2006.

21. Ehrman 2011.

Chapter Four—The Synoptic Take(s) on Jesus

1. Boring 2006: 40.

2. Ibid. 41.

3. Levison 868.

4. Collins 2007: 453.

5. See Philip S. Johnston, "Gehenna," *NIDB* 2.531.

6. See Bauckham 1998: 39–44.

7. Bauckham 1998; Clark-Soles 2006.

8. Carey 2012: 53–54.

Chapter Five—Beyond the Synoptic Gospels

1. Kloppenborg 2008; but see Eve 2011; Goodacre 2002.
2. Kloppenborg 2008: 73–79.
3. Ibid. 80–84.
4. Green 1997: 463–64.
5. Nelson, *NIDB* 6.675.
6. Kloppenborg 1987; see Allison 1997.
7. Parsenios 2010.
8. Goodacre 2012.

Chapter Six—The Big Show

1. Friesen 2001.
2. *Epistles* 10.96-97.
3. deSilva 2009: 61.
4. Ibid. 58–63.
5. Craig R. Koester 2014: 680.
6. Huber 2007.

Chapter Seven—Epilogue

1. Keith 2014.
2. Swartley 2006: 189–253; Gorman 2015: 142–211.
3. Burns 360.
4. Pagels 2012.
5. Jones *et al.* 2014.
6. Boyer 1992: 139–40.
7. Smolenski 2000: 55–61; Nancy Koester 1995: 138–39.
8. Newport 2006.

Glossary

Antiochus IV Epiphanes—the Greek-speaking ruler of the Seleucid Empire based in Syria who ruled from 175 to 164 BCE; Antiochus's suppression of traditional Judean customs, including sacrifice in the temple, provoked the Maccabean Revolt

apocalyptic discourse—the flexible array of concepts and literary devices associated with the Jewish and Christian literary apocalypses

apocalypse—a literary genre providing the narrative of a visionary who undergoes a mystical experience that discloses otherworldly mysteries or the ultimate course of history

apocalypticism—social movements heavily influenced by apocalyptic discourse, particularly expectation concerning the imminent close of history

chiliasm—the imminent expectation of Christ's return to rule the world for a thousand years

Dead Sea Scrolls—a collection of documents, first discovered at Qumran, that includes both biblical and extrabiblical Jewish literature

dispensational premillennialism—the belief that according to the Bible God has divided history into seven periods, or dispensations, culminating in the following sequence of events: the return of Jesus to take believers into heaven, seven years of global conflict and suffering, and the return of Jesus to administer judgment and bring about a final era of salvation

Glossary

eschatology—discourse concerning ultimate things, whether the realms of heaven and hell, the fate of mortals beyond death, the final judgment, or the resolution of history

First Jewish Revolt—a revolt against Roman rule, 66–70 CE, that began with initial success but ended with the destruction of Jerusalem and its temple

Gnosis—the Greek word for knowledge; with respect to Christianity, refers to forms of Jesus devotion that promoted esoteric and mystical knowledge as a means of salvation

inaugurated eschatology—the belief that the life and resurrection of Jesus has inaugurated the realization of the kingdom of God, which must await its consummation upon Jesus's return

kingdom (or empire) of God—the active and effective exercise of God's rule over human affairs; the term often functions in contrast to the rule of present empires

L material—content unique to the Gospel of Luke

M material—content unique to the Gospel of Matthew

Maccabean Revolt—a Judean revolt from 167 to 164 BCE that ended Seleucid control of Judea and established Judean self-governance that endured just over a century

Marcan Priority—the hypothesis that the Gospel of Mark was composed before Matthew and Luke and that Matthew and Luke both derive their narrative framework and much of their content from Mark

messiah—literally, one who is anointed; in ancient Judaism and Christianity, a messiah is God's Chosen One who rules the world with justice

millennialism, or millenarianism—originally synonymous with chiliasm, the term has expanded to include the imminent expectation of a utopian future

Nag Hammadi Library—a library of ancient texts discovered in 1945 outside the Egyptian town of Nag Hammadi; includes twelve codices (volumes bound with a spine and cover) and over fifty independent literary works, all written in Coptic, that provide our most important primary sources for conversations regarding Gnosis-oriented Christianity

parousia—the transliteration of a Greek word that means *arrival*; refers to the second coming of Jesus

proto-apocalyptic literature—a term used to characterize Hebrew prophetic literature featuring concepts and literary devices that later mark the Jewish apocalypses

pseudepigraphy—literary forgery, a characteristic shared by most of the literary apocalypses, which ascribe themselves to great figures of the past

Q—a hypothetical source that consists of material shared by Matthew and Luke but not by Mark; the Q hypothesis assumes that the authors of Matthew and Luke alike shared and relied upon the Gospel of Mark, then attempts to explain how Matthew and Luke can share other content as well

rapture theology—the belief that near the end of time Jesus will return to gather believers, both living and dead, to meet him in the air and deliver them from this earth

realized eschatology—the belief that the life and resurrection of Jesus have brought about the kingdom of God in its fullness and that believers already enjoy the fullness of God's eschatological blessings

redaction—the process of editing; in this context, refers to the ways in which the authors of Matthew and Luke appropriated and modified Mark's narrative

resurrection—involves the transformation of dead persons to an embodied eternal life

Son of Man—an eschatological figure who governs human affairs and judges wickedness; can be synonymous with *messiah*

Synoptic Gospels—the Gospels of Matthew, Mark, and Luke, which share a basic narrative framework

Subject Index

afterlife, 4, 5–7, 16, 19–20, 23–24, 34, 38, 39, 47–48, 52–58, 61, 63–70, 89–90, 95, 104, 142–43, 149–51
alternative reality, 14–15, 23, 151–52
angels (including Satan and demons), 4–6, 10, 11, 13, 16, 20, 27, 32, 33, 34–40, 48, 77–79, 82–83, 88, 90, 94, 98, 101, 103, 106–11, 114, 123, 127, 137–38, 149
antichrist, 114
Antiochus IV, 8–9, 28–30
apocalypses (literary), 1, 3, 4, 7–9, 12, 17, 26–30, 33–35, 65, 113–16, 122, 131, 133–35, 138, 140, 142–45
apocalyptic discourse, 1–2, 6–7, 9–17, 20, 21, 26, 30, 39–40, 46, 47, 58–61, 70, 76–77, 82, 92–94, 98, 101, 106–11, 133–35, 137–45
apocalyptic eschatology, 12, 17, 38, 46, 59–60, 65–70, 75, 76–77, 87–89, 92, 98, 100, 104, 106, 110–11, 137, 141
apocalyptic literature (defined), 9–12
apocalyptic speculation, ancient, 12, 32, 34, 44, 80–81, 90–91, 97, 106–8, 145–46
apocalyptic speculation, contemporary, 12, 113–114, 145–47
apocalypticism, 1, 5, 10–12, 26, 44, 110–111, 144–47
apostasy, end-time, 34, 68–70, 87
authority, in apocalyptic literature, 14, 21, 49–51, 59, 70, 81, 93, 94, 107, 114, 115, 128, 135, 139

battle, eschatological, 25
beast(s), 14, 29, 36, 114, 115–17, 119, 121–22, 124, 127–35, 140, 142, 147, 148

Bible prophecy movement, 12, 113–14, 144–47
Branch Davidians, 11, 146–47
Bride, in Revelation, 123, 130–31

calendar, 9, 33
Calvin, John, 146
chiliasm, 10–12
crisis, end-time, 11, 15, 20–22, 52, 70, 87, 114

Dead Sea Scrolls, 3, 11, 26–27, 30–32, 74
determinism, 15–16
dispensational premillennialism, 145–47
dualism, 15–16, 25, 31–32, 34–35, 138–39

eschatology, inaugurated versus realized, 66–70, 104–5, 108
Essenes, 11–12, 47, 74
ex eventu prophecy, 13–14

Gehenna, 84
German Peasants' Revolt, 11, 146
Gnosis, Gnosticism, 144–45
Gospels, canonical, 12, 14, 16, 17, 22, 43, 73–96, 121

heaven, heavens, 15, 23, 34–35, 49, 61, 75, 77–78, 80, 83, 86, 88, 92, 93, 94, 105, 107, 111, 113, 114, 115, 116, 123–124, 130–31, 135, 138, 143–44, 150
heavenly intermediary, interpreting angel, 13, 20, 22–23, 33, 35, 36–38
hell, 15, 57–58, 61, 84, 103, 107, 113, 138–39, 143

Subject Index

Holy Spirit, 34, 56, 61, 64, 75–77, 85, 88, 92–93, 98, 107

imperial cults, Roman, 121–22, 124, 128

Jesus, 10, 12, 15, 16, 40, 43, 44–45, 62–63, 73–111, 113–14, 115, 116, 118, 121, 123–24, 126, 127, 131, 132, 133, 135, 137–50
- baptism of, 55, 73–78, 82–83, 85, 88, 94, 97, 107, 111, 139
- crucifixion of, 6, 44, 52–57, 59, 70, 79, 81, 87, 94, 98–99, 101, 102, 107, 109, 123, 124, 140, 143
- resurrection of, 4, 6–7, 44, 52–57, 59–60, 66–70, 79, 81–82, 87, 94, 98–99, 101, 107–11, 137–38, 143
- return of, *parousia*, 7, 14–15, 17, 24, 27, 44, 52–57, 59–60, 63–65, 66–70, 80–81, 86–88, 90–91, 94–95, 99–102, 107–11, 113–14, 137–38, 148

John the Baptist, 44–45, 73–75, 82–83, 85, 88, 89, 94, 97–98, 103, 107–9, 111

Joseph, 26

Josephus, 4, 48, 155n4, 157n9

judgment, final, 5–6, 15–17, 26, 28, 34–35, 44, 57–58, 60, 61, 62, 65, 74, 80, 84–90, 94–95, 98–101, 103, 106–11, 114, 137, 142, 149

kingdom of God, 29, 33, 44, 62, 77–78, 82–86, 88–89, 92, 94, 97, 101, 102, 103, 105, 107, 108, 111, 121, 139, 141, 160

Koresh, David, 146–47

Latter-day Saints, 11

Lindsey, Hal, 146

Luther, Martin, 146

Merkabah mysticism, 25

messiah, 3, 5–7, 28, 32, 34–35, 37, 38–39, 76–81, 92, 102, 106–8, 126, 141, 149

millennialism, or millenarianism, 10–12, 144–47

Miller, William, 11, 146

Mormon, Book of, 11

Nero, 118–19, 121, 130, 134

parables of Jesus, 5, 85–86, 90, 102, 106, 140

Paradise, 49

Paul, 10, 12, 13, 14, 15, 16, 17, 24, 34, 40, 43–72, 76, 82, 88, 93–94, 108–9, 111, 115, 121, 137, 142, 147, 148, 149, 150

Paul, disputed and undisputed letters of, 46

Peoples Temple, 11

persecution, 9, 40, 44, 63, 80, 87, 93, 118–22, 142–43

Pharisees, 44, 47–48

prophetic literature, Hebrew, 15, 20–26, 33, 115, 138

Prostitute, Whore, Babylon, of Revelation, 121, 124, 129–30, 132, 133, 134

Proto-apocalyptic literature, 19–26, 138

pseudonymity, 13, 30, 46, 65–70

Q, 44–45, 73–74, 85, 88, 97–100, 108–11

rapture theology, 113–14, 144–47

resistance, apocalyptic literature as, x, 17, 29–30, 118, 128, 139–41, 146, 148, 149

resurrection, 4, 5–7, 16, 23–24, 34, 38, 39, 47–48, 52–58, 82, 87, 89–90, 92, 95, 104, 108–11 137, 149–51

revolt, Maccabean, 9, 13–14, 28–30, 33, 139, 147

revolts, Jewish, 8–9, 14, 35, 80, 88, 117–18

rhetoric, apocalyptic, x, 58–60, 131–33, 139, 147–48

rhetoric, Greco-Roman, 50, 53, 58

Rome, 8, 14, 20, 35–36, 44, 45, 79–80, 93, 117–19, 121–22, 125, 128–34, 140–41, 145–49, 151

rulers of this age, 53

Subject Index

Sadducees, 4, 6, 24, 47–48
salvation, savior, 3, 39, 59, 61–63, 64, 65, 66, 67, 68, 70, 75, 77, 89, 103, 105, 107, 109
Satan, or devil, 4–6, 34, 48, 49, 69, 77, 79, 82, 88, 94, 98, 99, 101, 103, 104, 106–11, 118, 121, 123, 126–28, 137, 139, 149
Septuagint, 27
Smith, Joseph, 11
Son of God, 76–77, 79, 94, 102, 107
Son of Man, 3, 7, 15, 25, 27–28, 36, 77, 79–81, 86, 87, 91, 94, 99–100, 102, 137, 141, 148
symbols, symbolism, 14, 114
Synoptic Problem, 73–74, 82–83, 91, 97–101

throne, divine or heavenly, 15, 20, 25, 35, 77, 80, 86, 123, 140
tours of heaven and hell, 16, 20, 23
tribes, Israel's twelve, 34, 37, 99–100, 111

universalism, 61–63

visions, 20–26, 29–30, 33, 36–38, 48–51, 82, 93–95, 97, 107, 114–17, 123, 133, 135, 138–39, 142, 143, 144–45, 149–50

Watchers, 33
wisdom literature, 26, 29, 65, 100, 110, 138
wisdom, mantic, 26
wrath of God, 52, 57–58, 61–62, 103, 138

Author Index

Allison, Dale C., 70, 112, 156, 157, 158
Aune, David, 118, 136

Bassler, Jouette M., 70, 157
Bauckham, Richard, 17, 95, 155, 157
Beker, J. Christiaan, 70
Beyerle, Stefan, 40, 156
Blount, Brian K., 95
Boring, M. Eugene, 75, 95, 157
Boyarin, Daniel, 70, 156
Boyer, Paul, 152, 158
Bremmer, Jan N., 40, 156
Brown, Alexandra R., 71
Brown, Raymond E., 67
Burns, Dylan M., 144, 152, 158

Campbell, Douglas M., 71
Carey, Greg, 18, 40, 71, 95, 136, 155, 156, 157
Carter, Warren, 95, 136
Charlesworth, James H., 71, 157
Clark-Soles, Jaime, 18, 96, 155, 157
Collins, Adela Yarbro, 18, 155
Collins, John J., 17, 41, 155, 156, 157
Cook, Stephen L., 41, 156
Cox, Daniel, 152
Croy, C. Clayton, 81

De Boer, M. C., 71, 157
deSilva, David A., 41, 126, 136, 155, 156, 158
Dunn, James D. G., 71, 157

Ehrman, Bart D., 143, 157
Eve, Eric C. S., 112, 158

Friesen, Steven J., 136, 158
Frykholm, Amy Johnson, 152

Gaventa, Beverly Roberts, 71, 157
Goff, Matthew, 41, 156
Goodacre, Mark, 112, 157
Gorman, Michael J., 152, 158
Grabbe, Lester L., 41, 156
Green, Joel B., 96, 158

Hart, Trevor, 17
Hill, Craig C., 18
Himmelfarb, Martha, 18, 41, 156
Horsley, Richard A., 18
Huber, Lynn R., 136, 158

Johnston, Philip S., 157
Jones, Robert P., 152, 158

Keith, Chris, 153, 155, 158
Kloppenborg, John S., 100–101, 112, 156, 158
Koester, Craig R., 136, 158
Koester, Nancy, 153
Kraybill, J. Nelson, 136

Levenson, Jon D., 41, 156
Levison, John R., 96, 112, 157

Martínez, Florentino García, 31
Martyn, J. Louis, 71
Meeks, Wayne A., 71, 157
Myers, Ched, 96

Navarro-Rivera, Juhem, 152, 158
Nelson, R. D., 96, 158

Author Index

Newport, Kenneth G. C., 153, 158
Newsom, Carol A., 41, 156

O'Leary, Stephen D., 17, 155

Pagels, Elaine, 153, 158
Parsenios, George L., 112, 158
Portier-Young, Anathea, 29–30, 156

Reddish, Mitchell G., 143
Rhoads, David, 136
Richter, Amy E., 18, 155
Roetzel, Calvin, 71, 156

Segal, Alan F., 17, 41, 155, 156, 157

Smolenkski, Reiner, 153, 158
Stein, Stephen J., 17, 155
Swartley, Willard M., 153, 158
Sweeney, Marvin A., 41, 156

Taylor, Walter F., 71, 156

VanderKam, James C., 42, 156
Vermes, Geza, 31

Wessenger, Catherine, 153
Wills, Lawrence M., 42, 156
Wright, Benjamin G., III, 42, 156
Wright, N. T., 18, 71, 155, 157

Index of Ancient Sources

Ancient Near Eastern Literature

Baal epic 25

Enuma Elish 25

Epic of Gilgamesh 20

Greco-Roman Literature

Iliad 20

Josephus, *Antiquities*
18.1.3 . . . . 157n9
18.1.14 . . . . 155n4

Josephus, *War*
2.8.14 . . . . 155n4, 157n9

Pliny the Younger
Epistles 10.96-97 158

Tacitus, *Annals*
15.44 119

Hebrew Scriptures

Genesis 150
2 135
2:9 135
2:10 135
5:24 30
6:1-4 . . . . 16, 27, 33
12:1-3 92
37 127
37–48 26
49 33

Leviticus
12:1-2 33

Numbers
1:49-50 33
25:1-9 125
31:16 125

1 Samuel
16:14 5

2 Samuel
7:4-29 3

1 Kings
3:6 3
8:23-26 3
16–21 125

2 Kings
1:8 73
9 125

1 Chronicles
21:1 4

Job
1–2 4

Psalms
2 3
9:4, 7 25
11:4 25
29 25
68:4 148
89 3
93:2 25
97 25
104:3 148
110:1 141

Index of Ancient Sources

Isaiah 20–21
1:1 21
6:1-13 . . . . 20, 25
9. 3
11. 3
24–27. 22
24:17-23 20
24:21-23 22
26:19 4
40:3 74
42. 3
61. 3
66:18-24 92

Jeremiah
7:30-34 84
11:1-3 21
13:1-11 23
19:1-13 84

Ezekiel. 20–21
1:1 . . . . 25, 75, 77
14:14, 20 30
28:3 30
37. . . . . 20, 77
37:1-14 23–24
37:11 23
38–39. 22
40–48. 20, 23, 32
47:13–48:35. 100

Daniel 4, 7, 8–9, 20–21,
    26–30, 115, 132, 137, 139, 142, 147
1-6. 28–30
2:4b–7:28. 28–30
2:44 29
7. . . . . 3, 14, 28, 30, 80, 116, 128
7–12. . . . . 4, 27–30
7:3-8 128
7:13 . . . . 28, 141, 148
7:13-14 79
7:27 29
8:19 13
9:24 20
9:25 14
9:27 . . . . 69, 80
10:4 77
10:7 75
11. . . . . 14, 28
11:31 . . . . 69, 80
11:33-35 26
12. 16
12:1-3 . . . . 4, 5, 24, 149
12:1-10 26
12:11 . . . . 69, 80

Hosea 127, 131

Joel 20–21
2:1-2 20
2:10 22
2:28-29 76
2:28-32 . . . . 89, 93

Amos
7–9. 23

Obadiah
1:1 21

Nahum
1:1 21

Zechariah 20–21
1-8. 23
1:7–6:8. . . . . 20, 23
3:1-2 4
12–14. 20
14:2-4 22

Malachi
3:1 74

Apocrpypha

Wisdom of Solomon
4:20–5:23. 26

Daniel, Additions to (Prayer of Azariah, Susanna, Bel and the Dragon) 27

1 Maccabees
1:54 80

Jewish Pseudepigrapha (and Christian versions)

Abraham, Apocalypse of 34, 35

2 Baruch 3, 7, 9, 26,
    34, 35, 140, 142

Index of Ancient Sources

3:1-9 38
4:1-7 38
5:1-4 38
11:1-3 38
13:5-12 38
14:4-7 38
15:1-8 38
27 38
28–30 38
31–34 38
36–40 38
42:5 39
44–46 38
53–74 38
77–87 38
77:13-16 39

3 Baruch 7, 9, 34, 35

Book of the Giants 27

1 Enoch 3, 7, 8–9, 13, 26–30,
     31, 33, 34, 39, 79–80, 137, 139, 142, 147
Watchers, Book of the (chs. 1–36) . . 16, 26, 139
Parables of Enoch (chs. 37–71) 28, 141
Astronomical Book (chs. 72–82) . . . 27, 139
Dream Visions (chs. 83–90) . . . 27–28, 30, 39
Animal Apocalypse (chs. 85–90) 13, 14,
     133–34, 139
Epistle of Enoch (chs. 91–105) . . . 27–28, 30
Apocalypse of Weeks (91:11-17; 93:1-10) . . . 29
21–22 16
49:2-3 76
54:5-6 8
94:69 141
98:3 8
106–108 27

2 Enoch 27
20:3 34

3 Enoch 27

4 Ezra 3,
     7, 8, 9, 13, 21, 26, 35, 79–80, 140, 142
4:12 36
4:22-25 36
7:130 21
9:26–10:59 36
11:5 36
11:37–12:3 133
11:39-40 36
11:41-42 36
12:31-34 37
13:2-4 37
13:5-13 37
13:32 37
13:52 37
14:1-6 37
14:27-35 37
14:42 21
14:45-47 37
14:45-48 49

Isaiah, Ascension of
4:1-14 119

Jubilees 9, 27, 31, 32–34
1:4, 29 33
2:2 33
2:9 33
3:9-14 33
4:16-26 33
5:1-11 33
17:15-18 34
23:11-31 34
30:18-20 33–34
31:11-17 33–34
48:9-19 34

Psalms of Solomon
17:37 76

Sibylline Oracles
5.137-154 119

Testaments of the Twelve Patriarchs . . . 27,
     33–35
Testament of Levi 2-5 34–35
Testament of Levi 2:11 35
Testament of Levi 8 34
Testament of Levi 18:7-12 76
Testament of Judah 24:1-2 34
Testament of Naphtali 6 34
Testament of Joseph 19

Dead Sea Scrolls

1QpHab (*Habakkuk Pesher*) . . 31, 139–40

1QM (*War Rule*) 32, 139–40

Index of Ancient Sources

1QS (*Community Rule*) 31
8:13-15 74

11Q15 (*Hymns*) 32

11QTemple (Temple Scroll) 23, 32

CD (*Damascus Document*) 31

New Testament

Matthew 3–4, 73–74, 82–98, 107–8, 147
3:7 85
3:10 85
3:11 .... 85, 106
3:16 83
4:1-11 4
4:17 82
4:23-25 84
5–7 84
5:1-12 101
5:3 .... 110, 111
5:22 84
5:34-37 110
5:43-47 102
5:48 109
6:19-20 111
7:1 111
7:7 110
7:16 110
7:19 84
7:21 110
7:21-23 .... 84, 86
8:11-12 .... 99, 101
8:12 .... 5, 85
9:32-34 5
9:34 4
10:1 5
10:28 99
10:38 98–99
11:21-23 99
12:18-27 24
12:22-30 99
12:38-42 99
12:42 99
13 85–86
13:24-30 .... 5, 85
13:36-43 .... 5, 64, 85
13:42 .... 8, 85
13:47-50 .... 5, 85
13:49-50 64
13:50 .... 8, 85
13:53-58 89
15:1-20 126
15:22 5
17:14-21 5
19:28 99
19:30 101
20:16 101
21:21 110
22:1-14 86
22:13 .... 5, 85
22:23-33 4
23:12 110
24 .... 87, 90, 141, 143
24–25 102
24:3 87
24:6 14
24:9 87
24:10-13 87
24:14 87
24:15 69
24:21 15
24:26-28 99
24:29 .... 15, 148
24:30 .... 25, 27, 148
24:32-33 143
24:34 .... 15, 147
24:34-35 106
24:36 86
24:37-42 114
24:40-41 99
24:42-44 60
24:51 .... 5, 85
25:1-13 86
25:25-36 110
25:30 .... 5, 85
25:31-46 .... 5, 64, 86
25:41 .... 4, 8
26:63-64 141
26:64 .... 25, 27, 148
27:11 141
27:29 141
27:37 141
27:42 141

27:51-53	89
27:51-54	87
27:52	6
27:52-53	64–65

Mark 73–98, 107–8, 147
1:1	76, 79
1:4	73, 78
1:7	74
1:8	85
1:10	83
1:10-11	76
1:12-13	77
1:14-15	83, 88
1:15	77, 78
1:21-28	77, 83, 84
1:23-24	78
1:32-34	83
1:34	78
1:38-39	83
1:40-45	79
2:1-12	79
2:10	81
2:28	81
3:11	77, 78
3:21-31	79
3:22	78
4.	85
5:7	77, 78
5:21-43	82
5:24-34	79
6:1-6a	89
6:7-13	78
7:19	126
7:24-30	79
8:21	79
8:29	77
8:31	81, 82
8:33	79
9:1	78
9:7	77–78
9:31	81, 82
9:43-47	85
10:33-34	81, 82
12:1-12	85
12:18-27	4
12:40	85
13	80–81, 90, 102, 141
13:2	80
13:6	90
13:7	14, 90
13:8	90
13:14	69, 80
13:19	15
13:20	91
13:24	15, 148
13:24-26	23
13:24-27	80
13:26-27	114
13:27	80
13:30	15, 80, 147
13:30-35	80
13:32	77, 79
14:28	82
14:50	79
14:61-62	77–78, 141
14:62	25, 27, 79, 80, 148
15:2	141
15:9	141
15:12	141
15:17-18	141
15:26	141
15:38	76
15:38-39	76–78
15:39	76–77
16:1-7	82
16:8	79, 81–82

Luke 6–7, 73–74, 88–98, 107–8, 147
3:1-22	88
3:7	85
3:9	85, 88
3:10	85
3:12	85
3:16	85, 89, 106
3:16-17	88
3:21-22	88
4:1-13	88
4:14-15	88
4:16-20	137
4:16-30	89
6:9	89
6:20	110, 111
6:20-26	101

Luke (cont.)
6:27-35 102
6:37 111
6:46 110
7:50 89
8:36 89
8:48 89
9:57-62 91
10:13-15 99
11:9 110
11:14-23 99
11:29-32 99
11:31-32 99
12:4-5 99
12:16-21 106
12:33-34 111
13:28 85
13:28-29 99
13:28-30 101
14:11 110
14:15-24 .... 85, 91
14:27 98
16:19-31 .... 64, 90
16:22-26 6
17:6 110
17:17-20 139
17:19 89
17:20-21 88
17:24 92
17:27-37 99
17:34-35 114
19:9 89
19:11 92
19:12-27 86
21 .... 102, 141
21:5-38 90–91
21:7 90
21:8 90
21:9 .... 14, 90
21:10-11 90
21:20 69
21:24 91
21:25 148
21:27-28 91
21:32 147
21:32-33 106
21:34-36 91

22:28-30 99
22:67-69 141
23:2-3 141
23:37-38 141
23:43 .... 6, 49, 64, 90
24:16 6
24:21 6
24:22-24 6
24:26 7

John 90, 97–111
3:17-21 103
3:19 103
3:36 .... 103, 104
4:14 104
4:25-26 102
5:21 104
5:22-30 .... 103, 104
5:28-29 90
6:39-54 24
6:47-54 104
7:20 103
8:44 103
8:48-52 103
8:50 103
8:51 104
9:22 102
9:39 103
10:20-21 103
11:24 90
11:25-26 104
12:31 103
12:48 103
13:2 103
13:27 102
13:34-35 102
15:6 103
15:12-17 102
16:2 102
16:11 103
18:33–19:22 141

Acts 45–46, 92–94, 121
1:8 92
2:16-18 76
2:17-18 89
2:17-21 92–93
2:20 148

Index of Ancient Sources

2:22-36 92
3:18-26 92
3:24 93
7:59 64
9. . . . . 50–51, 93
10–11. 126
10:1-9 94
10:13 93
10:15 93
10:34-43 92
11:5-14 94
11:26 40
13:38-41 93
15. . . . . 51, 126
15:7-9 94
22:6-11 94
23:6 47
23:6-10 47–48
23:8 4
26:5 47
26:12-20 94
26:19-23 92
26:28 40

Romans 52, 54, 57, 66
1:18-32 58
1:26-27 54
2:5 . . . . 57, 58
2:5-10 61–62
5:9 57-58
5:12-21 58
5:14-18 62
5:14-22 62
6–8. 55–57
6:1 56
6:4 67–68
6:4-5 . . . . 52, 56
6:5 57
8. 61
8:10-11 61
8:11 57
8:18-19 57
8:18-30 67
8:21 61
8:22-23 57
8:23 . . . . 57, 61, 76
8:31-39 57

9:22 62
14–15. 126
14:1–15:13. 132
14:10-12 60
15:23-28 58
16:25 57

1 Corinthians 9–10, 52, 54, 57, 59, 63–64,
66, 139, 147
1-2 53
1:5-7 67
1:6-8 53
1:7 57
1:7-8 14
1:10-12 . . . . 59, 139
1:18 61
1:23 53
2:2 53
2:7-8 . . . . 53, 59
4:1-5 60
4:5 10
5:1-13 54
5:9 142
6:2-3 10
6:9-10 62
6:12-20 54
7. 54
8. 126
8:1 67
8:1-13 132
8:4 125
10. 126
10:11 138
10:14–11:1. 132
11. 126
12–14. 59
13:1-3 67
13:8-12 . . . . 59, 67
13:9-12 10
13:12 61
14:5-6 48
14:26 48
15:1-58 . . . . 6, 9–10, 53, 59, 67, 151
15:12-28 149
15:19 61
15:20 56
15:20-28 61

1 Corinthians (cont.)
15:22 . . . . 62, 63
15:23 . . . . 56, 61
15:36 149
15:37-38 149
15:42-54 150
15:51 63
15:51-52 61
16. 53
16:1-4 58

2 Corinthians 48–50
1:12 58
1:15–2:4. 49
2:15 62
4:3 62
4:11 63
5:10 58
7:8 142
8–9. 58
11:1 50
11:1-15 48–50
11:4-5 59
11:16-23 50
12:1-10 8,
   15, 34, 49–50, 59, 139
12:9 13
12:11 . . . . 49, 50
12:14–13:10. 49

Galatians. 52
1:4 14
1:6-9 . . . . 49–50, 59
1:11–2:14. 50-51
1:12 . . . . 8, 59
1:15-16 59
1:15–2:1. 43
2. 126
2:2 . . . . 8, 59
2:10 58
2:19-20 52
5:12 50
5:21 62
6:7-9 58
6:14-15 52

Ephesians 65–70

Philippians 58
1:6 14
1:7 63
1:12-14 63
1:17 63
1:19-24 64
1:21 61
2:25-30 64
3:5 47
3:10 61
3:10-11 64
3:11-12 66
4:10-20 64

Colossians. 65–70

1 Thessalonians. 52, 63, 147
1:9-10 52,
   57–58, 63-64, 137–38
1:10 . . . . 14, 62
4:1-8 54
4:13-18 6,
   24, 59–60, 114 139
4:16-17 148
4:17 . . . . 25, 27, 61
5:1-11 . . . . 60, 63, 69

2 Thessalonians. 65–70
1:7-10 69
2:2 142
2:3 87
2:3-10 69
2:15 142
3:17 142

1 Timothy 65–70
4:1 87
4:1-3 69

2 Timothy 65–70
3:1-9 69
4:3-4 69

Titus 65–70

Hebrews 138
1:3 138
1:4-14 138
1:13 138
2:5-9 138
6:4-6 143
8:1 138

9:26-28 138	1:3-4 115
10:12 138	1:4 131
10:26-31 138	1:4-6 45
10:29 143	1:5 . . . . 121, 133, 149
11:37 143	1:7 . . . . 27, 148
12:2 138	1:9 . . . . 114, 121, 132, 133
	1:11 . . . . 13, 133
James 43,	1:12-20 . . . . 116, 123, 148
46, 109–11, 138	1:13-16 28
1:4 109	1:19 133
1:5 110	2–3. . . . . 116, 118–21, 131, 133, 135, 147
1:6 110	2:3 120
2:5 . . . . 110, 111	2:6 119
2:14 110	2:7 49
2:15 110	2:9 . . . . 118, 120
2:19 110	2:10 . . . . 120, 132
3:6 84	2:13 . . . . 120, 121, 132, 133
3:12 110	2:14 119
4:7 110	2:14-15 125
4:10 110	2:15 119
4:11-12 111	2:19 120
5:1-3 111	2:20-24 . . . . 119, 127
5:1-6 151	3:4 132
5:1-11 138	3:9 118
5:7-9 110	3:10 . . . . 120, 124
5:12 110	3:14 133
	4:1 . . . . 75, 113, 114
1 Peter 138	5:1-13 123–24
1:3-5 138	5:5 37
1:12 138	5:5-7 133
3:22 138	5:6 . . . . 14, 123
4:5 138	5:9 123
4:16 40	6. 14
	6:9 121
2 Peter 45, 46	6:9-10 . . . . 65, 132, 133
3:15-16 45	6:9-11 65
	6:10 124
Jude 43	6:11 132
14 13	6:12 148
14–15 . . . . 8, 27	7:4-8 100
	8:13 124
Revelation 1, 5,	9:2 148
7, 8, 9, 13, 14, 15, 27–28, 30,	9:5-6 124
46, 113–36, 144–51	9:20-21 124
1:1 . . . . 115, 131	10:4 . . . . 13, 49
1:1-2 135	11:1-2 117
1:1-4 21	11:7 121
1:2 133	
1:3 . . . . 20, 115, 131, 135	

Revelation (cont.)
11:8 117
11:10 124
12. . . . . 22, 127
12:7-9 127
12:9 . . . . 121, 127
12:11 . . . . 121, 133, 149
12:11-12 132
12:17 . . . . 121, 127, 132, 133
13:1 . . . . 14, 128
13:1-2 128
13:2 127
13:3 119
13:4 . . . . 127, 128, 132, 149
13:7 . . . . 121, 128
13:8 124
13:11-17 128
13:12 . . . . 119, 124
13:14 124
13:18 134
14:4 123
16 20
16:9-11 124
16:9–19:4 129
16:13 128
16:18-19 130
17:1-4 125
17:2 124
17:6 . . . . 121, 129
17:8 119
17:9 . . . . 128, 129
17:9-10 117
17:10 134
17:11 119
17:16 . . . . 130, 133
18:4 132
18:8-9 130
18:9-20 130
19 22
19:15 . . . . 133, 149
19:15-21 25
19:20 128
19:21 . . . . 133, 149
20 22
20:1-10 128
20:4 . . . . 121, 132, 133
20:8 25

20:11-15 65
20:13 150
21–22 . . . . 32, 131
21:1 106
21:3 131
21:5 133
21:9 123
21:10–22:5 23
21:11-21 131
21:12-14 100
21:24-25 131
21:27 131
22:1 135
22:2 . . . . 131, 135
22:6-21 114
22:7 115
22:7-19 20
22:18-19 . . . . 115, 135

Noncanonical Early Christian Literature

Acts of Paul & Thecla 45, 47

1 Clement 45–47

3 Corinthians 45

Hermas, Shepherd of 7, 9, 13, 30, 142–44, 151
6:4-8 143
17:3-5 141
22:5-10 142
31:1-7 143

Isaiah, Ascension of. 9, 21, 34, 143–44

Laodiceans, Epistle to the 45

Thomas, Gospel of. 6, 44-45, 97–111, 137
1 104
3 105
10 106
18 106
37 106
63 106
64 86

Paul, Apocalypse of 34, 45, 143

Peter, Apocalypse of 7, 9, 15, 143–44

www.ingramcontent.com/pod-product-compliance
Lightning Source LLC
Chambersburg PA
CBHW011718220426
43663CB00020B/2926